OH,
FOR
THE LOVE
OF
GOD

by

JOHN K. ANTONY

ISBN 978-0-692-25209-3

Book design by Andrea Mentzer
Jacket design by Andrea Mentzer
Edited by Sarah Whitman

For Kate Evertsen

TABLE OF CONTENTS

FOREWORD

•••

A priest's life is a busy one. Especially if he is pastor of a parish, he finds himself shifting gears all day long. William Martin writes that being a pastor is like being a stray dog at a whistler's convention! One moment he is celebrating morning Mass for the schoolchildren, the next moment consoling a grieving family who has lost a loved one, the next moment visiting the sick in the local hospital, the next moment meeting with the parish finance council and the next moment visiting with a young couple preparing for marriage. There is an essential and beautiful unity to his shifting of gears, however: The pastor does so in the midst of a community, this community, the one to whom the Lord has sent him as shepherd.

Preaching at Mass in a parish, then, never happens in a vacuum. A pastor knows his flock and loves them, and his preaching emerges both from his prayerful contemplation of Sacred Scripture and his prayerful contemplation of his people. Moving about in their midst from day to day, watching, listening and speaking with them, his heart is moved by the Lord and by them. The limitless experiences of human life and of the human heart give rise to limitless opportunities to reflect on the Word of God and how it sheds light on every human soul. The most frequent context for a priest's preaching is the Sunday Eucharist, when his parishioners gather with him to be fed by the Lord's Word and by his Body and Blood. In such a holy context, the Lord himself presides and proclaims his gospel through the ministry of the priest. Moreover, he does so in the midst of this assembly, for this people, at this time, and in this church.

The priest's homilies, therefore, are always a conversation of love — first, with God, and in God, with his parishioners. It is for that very reason that as he prepares to preach, the "gear-shifting" he does throughout the week informs and inspires what he might say. The priest himself is first a disciple of the Lord, and he needs the nourishment of the Word as much as anyone — perhaps even more. Thus, he preaches not as one who has all the answers, but as one who is a fellow pilgrim on the way, as a sinner who relies on the Lord's mercy, and as one who bears the Word but is not the Word himself. Throughout the week as he ministers to his parishioners, he not only seeks to meet their spiritual and pastoral needs, he very often discovers that from their faithful witness he learns the very lessons God is trying to teach him. Preaching does not happen in a vacuum, because a priest lives in a vital, breathing, growing, loving community of Christians, all of whom are seeking with him to know and serve the Lord.

In this collection of homilies, Fr. John K. Antony demonstrates what Pope Francis holds out in *The Joy of the Gospel* as one of the key characteristics of all Christian evangelizers: "They should appear as people who wish to share their joy, who point to a horizon of beauty and who invite others to a delicious banquet. It is not by proselytizing that the Church grows, but 'by attraction'" (No. 15). The great attraction of the Gospel is Jesus himself, because every homily should be prepared so that Jesus shines through the preacher. Even if the preacher possesses great oratorical skills, it is still Jesus who attracts, Jesus who calls, Jesus who saves. As St. Paul wrote to the Corinthians, "We do not preach ourselves but Jesus Christ as Lord, and ourselves as your slaves for the sake of Jesus. For God who said, 'Let light shine out of darkness,' has shone in our hearts to bring to light the knowledge of the glory of God on the face of Jesus Christ" (2 Corinthians 4:5-6). In the pages to come, you will see how many times Fr. Antony mentions the name of Jesus.

Fr. John has savored the Scriptures in prayer before putting pen to paper, and thus the insights that emerge from his preaching find easy resonance in the hearts of his congregation, and now, his readers. They sense in his words a distinctive recognition, and they say to themselves, "He knows us!" In fact, it is the Lord who knows us, the Lord who speaks to us, the Lord who loves us.

By its very nature, every celebration of the Eucharist is a commissioning, for at the dismissal the celebrant says to his people, "Go in peace, glorifying the Lord by your life." The same is true of every homily, for it should leave God's people with a desire to delve deeper into their faith, to take action, to respond. Pope Francis writes: "The preacher has the wonderful but difficult task of joining loving hearts, the hearts of the Lord and his people. The dialogue between God and his people further strengthens the covenant between them and consolidates the bond of charity. In the course of the homily, the hearts of believers keep silence and allow God to speak. The Lord and his people speak to one another in a thousand ways directly, without intermediaries. But in the homily they want someone to serve as an instrument and to express their feelings in such a way that afterwards, each one may choose how he or she will continue the conversation" (No. 143).

In the end, every preacher knows that he is caught up in a mystery, for God's word is alive and active. To preach the word is a privilege, a challenge and a cause for great humility. To be an instrument in the dialogue between God and his people causes the preacher to shake his head in wonder — and to take every homily, and every parishioner, to prayer. The homilies you are about to read reflect with joy the attraction of Jesus, the love of his Father and the guidance of the Holy Spirit.

Archbishop J. Peter Sartain
June 29, 2014
The Solemnity of Saints Peter and Paul

INTRODUCTION

...

People often ask me why I decided to become a priest. I always answer, "There was a pretty girl I really liked in the eighth grade. One day I asked her to go on a date with me. She said, 'No.' So, I figured I might as well become a priest." Humorous as that story may be — it wasn't very funny at the time — I've learned that God often speaks to us through other people. It wasn't that God hit me over the head and told me to become a priest. Rather, He nudged me in that direction through the answer of that young girl. This has happened again and again in my life: no sledgehammer blows, just gentle suggestions; to consider this college, to read that book, to attend this church, to try chai latte. Indeed, it was a simple suggestion of a friend that prompted me to write this book. In every conversation I've had, I've begun to perceive the presence of another, whom I believe is the Lord Jesus. The reason I became a priest is because Jesus spoke to me through that young girl (and a lot of other people), and I tried to listen.

This seems to me the essence of every effective homily or sermon: that it serves to enhance that silent but sacred conversation between Christ and a Christian. As each Sunday approaches, every preacher asks himself or herself the question (sometimes in desperation): "What am

I going to tell the people this Sunday?!" Instead, I suggest we preachers should ask ourselves, "What does Jesus want to tell the people this coming Sunday?" Our job in preaching is to facilitate that conversation in the heart between the believer and the Lord. Jesus reminded His disciples, "He who hears you, hears me" (Luke 10:16). Blessed John Henry Newman, a master preacher in his own right, described it more intimately saying, "cor ad cor loquitur" (heart speaks to heart). When a sermon hits home, it's because the message touched a person's heart, but what's more, the hearer could perceive behind the preacher's words the voice of Jesus Himself. Too bad that young girl in eighth grade didn't become a preacher; she gave a great sermon that day helping me to hear Christ speaking.

The following homilies are grouped into five chapters, each describing a different way the Lord has spoken to me, which may help you to hear how He's speaking to you. The first chapter is "Discipleship" because, before everything else, there is an encounter between the believer and Jesus. Everyone receives a call by Christ that is customized, tailor-made, for him or her. That first contact with Christ is as alluring and mysterious as the subtle smile on DaVinci's Mona Lisa inviting everyone for a closer look. Each homily in this chapter tries to make us more aware of that invitation to discipleship and to inspire us to answer more eagerly. The second chapter is called "Fellowship," and shows how other people often "translate" what Jesus has to say to us. Our relationship with the Lord very, very rarely consists of just "me and Jesus," but rather, almost always extends beyond me to "we and Jesus." Christian life is fellowship. The third chapter, called "Grace," describes how the Lord's voice can be heard everywhere: in every babbling brook, in each swallow's song, even in the whispering wind. This chapter invites us to open our ears to the grace-filled symphony of creation. The fourth chapter is entitled "Self-awareness." Anyone who has been alive as long as I have realizes we don't just learn about the world around us, but more importantly, we learn about ourselves. These homilies raise our awareness of growing in self-awareness. After many years of penetrating self-examination, St. Augustine finally concluded: "You have made us for yourself, O Lord, and our hearts are restless until they rest in Thee." The last chapter, "Discernment," perhaps deserves to be the first since understanding our Christian journey, figuratively holding a compass that points true north, logically comes before we can take the first step. But I've placed it last because true discernment combines the insights gained from "discipleship," "fellowship," "grace" and "self-awareness," and distills them into practical wisdom that guides our lives. Discernment, in other words, involves more than knowing the path; it requires having the courage to choose the path. Of course, when all is said and done, it doesn't really matter what any homily says or how they are grouped; it only matters what Jesus says to you in your heart. I urge you to listen.

When the prophet Samuel was a young apprentice (probably the age of an eighth grader) serving in the Temple under Eli, he also first heard the Lord calling him. Samuel mistakenly thought he had heard the voice of Eli and so ran to him. After making the same mistake for the third time, Eli wisely counsels Samuel, saying, "Go to sleep, and if you are called, reply, 'Speak, Lord, your servant is listening'" (1 Samuel 3:9). That's my advice to you as you read these homilies, and before you hear the homily or sermon this coming Sunday. Say in your heart, "Speak, Lord, your servant is listening."

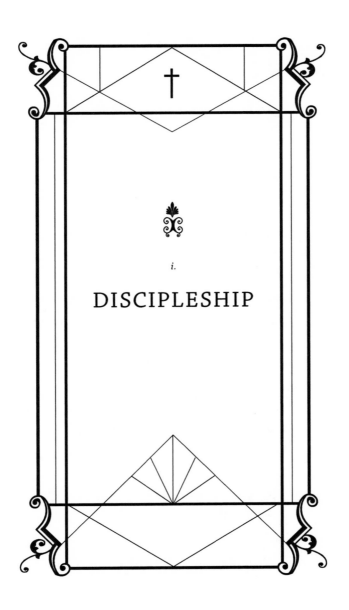

i.

DISCIPLESHIP

I am an organizational freak. I like my life compartmentalized into different times and places, persons and activities: Work doesn't overlap into worship, and I keep those two a safe distance from rest and relaxation. I don't even like my peas to touch my carrots on my plate! You would think a Catholic priest would cringe at our country's motto of "separation of church and state," but I nod approvingly. I happily raise a toast to Machiavelli, who advised, "Divide and conquer."

Christian discipleship, however, is exactly the opposite of my mindset. Instead of a life that's segregated and scattered, each part vying for attention and importance, discipleship involves integrating all the disparate and disjointed parts of one's life around a central axis. That central axis, of course, is Jesus. St. Paul urged the Colossians to have their relationship with Jesus as the principle and purpose of every aspect of their lives, saying, "And whatever you do, whether in word or deed, do it all in the name of the Lord Jesus" (Colossians 3:17). Discipleship doesn't seek to divide and conquer; it desires that every department of life be conquered by Christ.

Discipleship doesn't happen in a day, in one dramatic and decisive moment, not even for St. Paul who was knocked off his horse (cf. Galatians 1:18). Discipleship unfolds gradually. The great reformer Martin Luther noticed at least three stages of discipleship when he said, "There are three conversions: the conversion of the heart, the conversion of the mind and the conversion of the pocketbook." A former Augustinian monk, he was always the pragmatist. Luther was lamenting the lack of integration in the lives of Christ's disciples — even our wallets should be subject to Jesus! — and he pressed for a reform to make a relationship with Jesus the integrating principle in every disciple's life.

This chapter isn't intended to present an exhaustive list of the virtues of a disciple, but merely a cornucopia of qualities that should be woven into a Christian's life. The following homilies touch upon such diverse themes as foolishness and wisdom, holiness, sincerity in speech, the blessing of baptism and true joy, to name but a few. While these may seem random and unrelated, they comprise part of the kaleidoscope of Christian life that shines in brilliant colors only when illuminated by the light of Christ. As you read these homilies, listen to the Lord speaking in your heart. How is He inviting you to a deeper discipleship, combining and correlating work and worship, prayer and play, love and laughter?

EARLY LOVES

Remembering how we first fell in love with Jesus

•••

Matthew 4:18-23

As Jesus was walking by the Sea of Galilee, he saw
two brothers, Simon who is called Peter, and his brother Andrew,
casting a net into the sea; they were fishermen. He said to them,
"Come after me, and I will make you fishers of men."
At once they left their nets and followed him. He walked along
from there and saw two other brothers, James, the son of
Zebedee, and his brother John. They were in a boat, with their
father Zebedee, mending their nets. He called them, and
immediately they left their boat and their father and followed
him. He went around all of Galilee, teaching in their synagogues,
proclaiming the gospel of the kingdom, and curing every disease
and illness among the people.

We've all heard a lot about Pope Francis, but I want to share something about Pope Francis you probably don't know. Have you heard the story of how he decided to become a priest? As a young man growing up in Argentina, he had a close-knit group of friends whom he often went camping with. When he was 17 years old, he was on his way to join those friends for a picnic, when he walked by a church. A thought popped into his mind that he should go to confession. That confession changed his life. The priest who heard his confession was very spiritual and helped young Jorge Mario (the pope's real name) to experience God's mercy in a profound and permanent way. When he walked out of that church, Jorge Mario was a different man. He knew from that day he had to become a priest and tell other people about God's mercy.

Now, that's an interesting story; but it gets a lot better. The pope's only surviving sister remembered that young Jorge was deeply in love with a young lady in that same youth group, and that day at the picnic, he was actually going to propose to her, to ask her to marry him. Of course, he never did. The pope's sister wouldn't share any more details of that story, saying, "If I keep telling this story, my brother will end up excommunicating me!" Pope Francis has never forgotten that "early love." Oh, I'm not talking about his first love with that Argentinean beauty, but his first love with that Eternal Beauty, namely, Jesus. That "early love" that touched the pope when he was only 17 years old has stayed strong even now that Jorge Mario is 76 years old.

The gospel above relates two other stories about falling in love with Jesus, and how that "early love" leaves a lasting impact; it's like a rock thrown into a lake whose ripples reach the farthest shores of life. Jesus meets Peter and Andrew and simply says, "Come after me, I will make you fishers of men." And BOOM! They drop their nets and join Jesus for the rest of their lives. The second story unfolds similarly: Jesus meets James and John and the same thing happens again. The Bible says, "Immediately, they left their boat and their father and followed him." BAM! In one spellbinding second, they fall in love with Jesus. Anyone who says there's no such thing as love at first sight has never seen Jesus. Isn't this exactly what happened to the young Pope Francis? Sometimes an encounter with Christ is so revolutionary that you're willing to give up everything to be with Him: You'll give up your girlfriend, you'll sacrifice your promising professional career, you'll even turn your back on your mom and dad. I'm sure the apostles, like Pope Francis, often reflected on their first encounter with Christ, their "early love" — a rock thrown into the lake of their lives whose ripples would reach the farthest shores.

I first fell in love with Jesus while attending St. Theresa's elementary school in Little Rock, Ark.. Like Pope Francis, I, too, was in love with a young girl. But unlike the pope, when I asked her to go eat at Taco Bell, she said, "Heck no!" Do you think I need to work on my delivery? So, I pretty much HAD to fall in love with Jesus; I didn't have a choice! But I can remember how, during countless school Masses, I would stare at the large cross hanging over the altar. I was deeply moved by how much Jesus suffered and died for me. And a quiet question slowly surfaced in my mind: "What sacrifice can I make to show Jesus how much I love Him?" Suddenly, BOOM! I thought, "I know, I'll become a celibate priest!" To this day, I wonder, why didn't I think, "BOOM, I'll give up chocolate for Jesus?" But such is "early love" of the Lord. Maybe the pope has wondered once or twice, "What if I hadn't gone to confession that day?" Or the apostles had questioned, "What if we had ignored Jesus' call to become fishers of men?" But love defies all logic. The French Christian philospher Blaise Pascal famously said, "The heart has reasons that reason cannot know." You see, there is a deep mystery in falling in love, and when you fall in love with Jesus, the mystery is eternally deep. Perhaps that's why T.S. Eliot wrote in the poem "The Waste Land," "We shall not cease from exploration, and the end of all our exploring will be to arrive where we started and know the place for the first time." In other words, we should return again and again to our "early love" of Jesus — when and where and how we first fell in love with the Lord — and know it again as if for the first time.

Take a few minutes today to remember your "early love" of the Lord. When did you fall in love with Jesus? What did He say to you?

How did you respond to Him? How has that first encounter left a lasting impact on your life? How are you living your life today because of that early love? Or, have you forgotten that love? Many people, both Catholics and non-Catholics, fall in love with Jesus while attending a Catholic school, as I did: sitting in pews at daily Mass, or wearing plaid uniforms, or saying prayers before class or before lunch. That's the fundamental reason why Catholic schools exist: to help children to experience that "early love" of Jesus. Catholic schools are the spiritual equivalent of match.com and eHarmony, and we arrange a date with Jesus. And falling in love with Jesus is not some glib suggestion that you can just take or leave; it carries eternal consequences. The Book of Revelation begins with seven letters written to seven churches. The first letter is written to Ephesus, and harshly criticizes the Ephesians, saying, "But I hold this against you: You have forgotten your early love" (Rev. 2:4). They had forgotten how they first fell in love with Jesus. It is not a small matter to fall in love with the Lord, and it's an even more serious thing to forget that early love.

Shortly after his election, Pope Francis gave a lengthy interview. He was asked bluntly, "Who is Jorge Mario Bergoglio?" The Holy Father replied simply, "I am a sinner." Then the pope explained, "This is the most accurate definition [of me]. It is not a figure of speech, a literary genre. I am a sinner." Notice, he did not identify himself as the head of the Catholic Church, he didn't say he was a bishop or a priest, he didn't even say he was a Christian, but simply "a sinner." I think by saying that, he was remembering that 17-year-old boy, a young sinner who one day walked into a church in Buenos Aires and went to confession and fell in love with Jesus. The pope never wants to forget his "early love" because the ripples from that rock are still spreading to the farthest shores of his life.

GOD DISTRIBUTES THE LIGHTNING

Looking foolish out of love for Jesus

...

JEREMIAH 20:7

"You duped me, O LORD, and I let myself be duped; you were too
strong for me, and you triumphed. All the day I am an object of
laughter; everyone mocks me."

MATTHEW 16:21-23

Jesus began to show his disciples that he must go to
Jerusalem and suffer greatly from the elders, the chief priests,
and the scribes, and be killed and on the third day be raised.
Then Peter took Jesus aside and began to rebuke him, "God
forbid, Lord! No such thing shall ever happen to you." He turned
and said to Peter, "Get behind me, Satan! You are an obstacle to
me. You are thinking not as God does, but as human beings do."

One reason I like Shakespeare so much is his use of irony, where things
are not always as they seem, and the reality turns out to be the opposite
of its appearance. No character captures this quality quite like the Fool
in the play *King Lear*. Ostensibly, the Fool is just that: He's a clown,
comic relief, of no consequence. But when you look closer, the Fool

turns out to be the King's wisest counselor. He advises the King, "Have more than thou showest, Speak less than thou knowest, Lend less than thou owest, Ride more than thou goest, Learn more than thou trowest, Set less than thou throwest ... And keep in-a-door, and thou shalt have more, Than two tens to a score." For those who are not versed in Shakespeare's style, the Fool advises Lear to live temperately, modestly and humbly. Not bad advice from a Fool.

Something similar happened in the life of St. Thomas Aquinas. When he was a young novice monk, his monk-brothers used to make fun of him. They even named him the "Dumb Ox" because he was rather large in stature and didn't talk much. One day, three monks were at the monastery window and decided to play a trick on Thomas. As he walked by, they shouted, "Thomas, Thomas, come quick to the window! Cows are flying!" Thomas ran to the window and looked out, but of course, there were no winged cows. The three brothers laughed and laughed at how gullible Thomas was. But he quietly turned from the window and said, "I'd rather believe cows can fly than that brothers would lie." St. Albert the Great, a contemporary, said of Aquinas, "You can call him a Dumb Ox. But I tell you that the Dumb Ox will bellow so loud that his bellowing will fill the whole world." And it did. Aquinas is arguably the all-time greatest theologian. Things are not always what they seem, and those who seem the most foolish end up being the most wise.

In the Scripture readings above, Jeremiah and Peter struggle to learn this same lesson: The foolish are the wisest. Jeremiah complains, "You duped me, O Lord, and I let myself be duped ... All day long I am an object of laughter; everyone mocks me." In other words, I feel more foolish than the Fool in King Lear. I'm like Rodney Dangerfield, and "I don't get no respect." But in fact, Jeremiah would be one of the wisest prophets in the entire Old Testament. In the New Testament, Peter rebukes Jesus for wanting to go to Jerusalem and suffer and die.

He asks in effect, "Where's the wisdom in dying? Instead, flex your divine muscles and let the Romans see a little shock and awe!" But Jesus corrects him, saying, "You are thinking not as God does, but as human beings do." You see, Sacred Scripture, like Shakespeare, speaks about a sacred irony in the universe: Things are not what they seem; in fact, they are often the opposite. The fools end up being the wise, the weak turn out to be the strong, and to die is the only way to live truly.

Now, the easiest targets for foolishness are children, but ironically, they often end up being the wisest. Several years ago on Easter Sunday morning, the deacon of my church was preaching the children's sermon, and he reached into his bag of props and pulled out an egg. He pointed at the egg and asked the children, "Who can tell me what is inside this egg?" An eager little boy exclaimed, "I know! Pantyhose!" One family in my congregation recently related this story. They were visiting St. Joseph for the first time, and their small son watched as the usher passed around the offering plate. When they arrived near his pew, the boy said out loud, "Don't pay for me, Daddy, I'm under 5!" Little did he know at St. Joseph little children pay for themselves, not their daddies. Children can show us that same irony as Shakespeare and the Scriptures: The foolish are often the wisest.

Have you ever felt a little foolish in following Christ? I bet you have. And if you haven't, maybe you need to follow Jesus a little more closely. Every young man or woman who has considered a vocation as a priest or sister has felt that fear of foolishness. Who but a fool would give up everything to serve others?! Some people joke about handsome priests by calling them "Father-what-a-waste," implying that they could have done so much more with their lives, rather than waste it on being a poor priest. So, we priests and sisters can feel a little foolish. Married couples who don't use contraception and are open to a large number of children feel a little foolish because society says you should only have 1.5 children. (By the way, how do you have 1.5 children?) Having a large Catholic family used to be a badge of honor, but now it's the butt of jokes. When you pay your taxes faithfully and freely, while others look for loopholes, you feel a little foolish. When all your friends are having sex before marriage, but you choose to stay chaste, you feel a little foolish. When you don't have the designer clothes or the designer car or the designer body because you give your money to church and charity, you might feel a little foolish. When you stay home to raise your children instead of pursuing a career, you can feel a little foolish. Don't worry, that's how I describe what I do: "Fr. John is a stay-at-home-dad." For all these times when you feel like the Fool in a Shakespearean play, remember what Jesus said in this gospel: "You are thinking not as God does, but as human beings do." You will feel an intense irony in walking closely with Christ, but that is of no matter. It it is the Christian fool who is the wisest.

Mark Twain once made this memorable quip about fools: "The trouble ain't that there are too many fools, but that the lightning ain't distributed right." That is, the lightning isn't hitting the fools like it should. Well, it's OK if Mark Twain thinks you are a fool. Just make sure that God doesn't think you are a fool; because, after all, God's the one distributing the lightning.

GRANDMA LOVES JESUS

Enthusiastically loving Jesus and others

•••

JOHN 21:15-19

When they had finished breakfast, Jesus said to Simon Peter,

"Simon, son of John, do you love me more than these?"

Simon Peter answered him, "Yes, Lord, you know that I love you."

Jesus said to him, "Feed my lambs."

He then said to Simon Peter a second time,

"Simon, son of John, do you love me?"

Simon Peter answered him, "Yes, Lord, you know that I love you."

Jesus said to him, "Tend my sheep."

Jesus said to him the third time, "Simon, son of John,

do you love me?"

Peter was distressed that Jesus had said to him a third time,

"Do you love me?" and he said to him, "Lord, you know

everything; you know that I love you." Jesus said to him,

"Feed my sheep. Amen, amen, I say to you, when you were

younger, you used to dress yourself and go where you wanted;

but when you grow old, you will stretch out your hands, and

someone else will dress you and lead you where you

do not want to go."

He said this signifying by what kind of death he would

glorify God. And when he had said this, he said to him,

"Follow me."

Recently, a fellow pastor gave me a book called *Twelve Keys to an Effective Church*. And I thought, "Really? I mean, are things that bad that I need a book on how to be a pastor?" But as I was reading along, I noticed there wasn't much I was doing right, until I got to the second key, which was visiting families, and figured, OK, I got this one down. But as I read the "10 foundational principles of the art of effective visitation," I realized I'm doing this all wrong, too. For example, one principle states, "Decide the exact time you plan to leave. Don't stay too long." Well, I usually stay as long as there is more beer in the fridge and the basketball game isn't finished. Why would I leave? In fact, there's one family I have visited many times, and as soon as I walk through the door, the 6-year-old girl runs to the fridge to bring me a beer. I'm so proud of that family!

Another principle urges, "Avoid asking more than two or three questions during the whole visit. The purpose of the visit is not an interrogation to discover information." Now, I'm happy to say I've done that — only two or three questions. With one family I visited recently, I asked, "Isn't that a new Lexus in your driveway? Don't you want to increase your building donation to show God how grateful you are?" Two questions and I was done! So, folks, you don't have to worry about me becoming as popular as Joel Olsteen or Rick Warren, or any church I'm at becoming a mega-church.

Now, even though I'm about as smooth as Barney Fife during a family visit, I do agree with the book that such visits are key. The lifeblood of any parish is relationships, and one of the first relationships is with your pastor. That relationship must be founded on caring and concern, with mutual respect and trust, and dare I even say love. Recently, I've found it very easy to say to some parishioners, "I love you," and some spontaneously say that to me. John 10 says the good shepherd knows his sheep and they know him, and he lays down his life for his sheep. In other words, the shepherd and sheep love each other. Leadership guru John Maxwell says, repeatedly, "People don't care how much you know until they know how much you care," how much you love. *Twelve Keys to an Effective Church* really is pretty good, but I am convinced that the main key to an effective church is love.

In the gospel above, Jesus tells Peter that the key to successful ministry as the pope is love, and above all, love for Jesus. So, Jesus asks Peter, "Simon, son of John, do you love me more than these?" The reason Jesus asked Peter the same question three times was to make up for Peter's three denials. But what's more intriguing to me is the phrase "more than these." There are at least two possible interpretations. First, Jesus is asking Peter, "Do you love Me 'more than these,' more than you love them?" That is, do you love Me more than you love your closest friends? And Peter unflinching says, "Yes." Second, Jesus is asking Peter, "Do you love Me 'more than these,' more than they love Me?" Is your love for Me greater than their love for Me? Again, Peter responds confidently, "Yes, Lord." You see, Jesus is testing Peter and preparing Peter for his future Petrine ministry, as the first pope, where he must be an example of love to the other apostles and indeed to the whole Church. That's why in Acts of the Apostles 5:29, Peter says boldly to the Jewish Sanhedrin, "We must obey God rather than men." He could say that because he loved Jesus "more than these." Peter loved Jesus more than anything, and that kind of love is the key to an effective church. Love for Jesus is the key to Christianity.

A parishioner shared with me a letter she received from her grandmother, who, like Peter, loves Jesus more than anything. I was so impressed. It read, "The other day I went up to a local Christian bookstore and saw a 'Honk if you love Jesus' bumper sticker. I was feeling pretty sassy that day because I had just come from a thrilling choir performance, followed by a thunderous prayer meeting, so I bought the sticker and put it on my car. Boy, I'm glad I did! What an uplifting experience followed! I was stopped at a light at a busy intersection, just lost in thought about the Lord and how good He is ... and I didn't notice the light had changed to green. It is a good thing someone else loves Jesus because if he hadn't honked, I'd never have noticed! I found that LOTS of people love Jesus! While I was sitting there, the guy behind me started honking like crazy, and then he leaned out of his window and screamed 'For the love of God! Go! Go! Jesus Christ! Go!' What an exuberant cheerleader he was for Jesus! Everyone started honking! I just leaned out of my window and started waving and smiling at all these loving people. I even honked my horn a few times to share in the love! There must have been a man from Florida back there because I heard him yelling something about a 'sunny beach.' I saw another guy waving in a funny way with only his middle finger stuck up in the air. I asked my teenage grandson in the backseat what that meant, and he said it was probably a Hawaiian good luck sign or something. Well, I've never met anyone from Hawaii, so I leaned out the window and gave him the good luck sign back. My grandson burst out laughing ... he was enjoying the religious experience, too! A couple of the people were so caught up in the joy of the moment that they got out of their cars and started walking toward me. I bet they wanted to pray or ask what church I attended, but this is when I noticed the light had changed. So, I waved to all my sisters and brothers grinning, and drove on through the intersection." Here comes the best part. Grandma wrote, "I noticed I was the only car that got through the intersection before the light changed red again, and I felt kind of sad that I had to leave them after all the love we shared, so I slowed the car down, leaned out the window and gave them all the Hawaiian good luck sign one last time as I drove away. Praise the Lord for such wonderful folks! Love, Grandma." Have you received a letter like that from your grandma?

I know that letter was over-the-top, but I believe our love for Jesus is going to make us Catholics look more and more like Grandma, out of step with the world around us. But if you love Jesus as much as Grandma did, you don't care. You see, like Peter, we have to love Jesus "more than these." The President and Congress are considering comprehensive immigration reform. Is our love for Jesus greater than our ideological or political preferences? Jesus asks us, "Do you love Me more than these ideas or even more than these laws?" Maybe we're harboring some hurt from a family member that we won't let go of, that we refuse to forgive. But do we love Jesus more than these grudges and wounds? Maybe our friends are a bad influence on us, leading us away from Christ into immoral activities, and we try to leave them. Jesus asks us, "Do you love Me more than these?" Do you ever wonder why the population of young people in Protestant churches is growing so greatly? It's because they see people like Grandma there, who love Jesus more than life itself. And those same young people unfortunately don't see such people madly in love with Jesus in the Catholic Church. So, Jesus is asking us Catholics, "Do you love Me more than these?" And if we reply bravely like Peter, Jesus gives us the grace we need. So that no matter what the circumstances of our life, we can say with Peter, "We must obey God rather than men."

I can't wait to read more of that book and see what else I'm doing wrong as a pastor. In the meantime, I'll just love you, and you just love me. And together, we'll try to love Jesus "more than these," more than everything, more than everyone.

ONLY GOD CAN MAKE A TREE

Believing in God in an atheistic culture

• • •

MARK 10:46-52

As Jesus was leaving Jericho with his disciples and a sizable crowd, Bartimaeus, a blind man, the son of Timaeus, sat by the roadside begging. On hearing that it was Jesus of Nazareth, he began to cry out and say, "Jesus, son of David, have pity on me." And many rebuked him, telling him to be silent. But he kept calling out all the more, "Son of David, have pity on me."
Jesus stopped and said, "Call him." So they called the blind man, saying to him, "Take courage; get up, Jesus is calling you."
He threw aside his cloak, sprang up, and came to Jesus. Jesus said to him in reply, "What do you want me to do for you?"
The blind man replied to him, "Master, I want to see."
Jesus told him, "Go your way; your faith has saved you."
Immediately he received his sight and followed him on the way.

Have you noticed something sinister is afoot in our society? Our culture is not just becoming less Christian, it is increasingly atheistic. That is, many people don't even believe in God, let alone in Jesus Christ. Two weeks ago, I stopped at a local gas station to fill up. When I walked into the store, the attendant was excitedly talking to a young man about 18 years old holding a skateboard. The attendant motioned my way and said, "Look, here's a priest, he'll tell you why there is a God!" I thought to myself: "Oh, brother, I hate walking into these situations." So, I turned to the young man and said, "Well, kid, there is a God." Then, I said to the attendant, "Can I get $30 on pump 4?" Seeing I was no help, the attendant kept talking to the teen. But I gotta say, I was impressed, because he said to the teen, "You know, some day, you're going to have a child. And the day you hold that baby in your arms, you'll know beyond the shadow of a doubt that there is a God." I thought, "Wow, that's better than what I would have said!" But I'll never forget that young man's answer. Without any emotion on his face, he said flatly, "Why would I want to bring another one of me into this world?" His reply blew me away. But that is at the heart of atheism: Not only do you deny God, but you also deny your own human dignity, your intrinsic worth. Genesis says we are created "in the image and likeness of God," and so we know we're good because we're created in the image of God who is goodness itself. But what if we deny there is a God? Then, we inevitably deprive the human person of his deepest dignity, his core goodness.

Richard Dawkins, an atheist who teaches at Oxford, made the same connection between God and man. He wrote, "An atheist ... is somebody who believes there is nothing beyond the natural, physical world, no supernatural creative intelligence lurking behind the observable universe," and then he added, "[and] no soul that outlasts the body." In other words, if you get rid of God, you also get rid of your own soul, your human dignity, your ultimate worth. That teenager at the gas station was right: If there's no God, "why bring another one of me into this world?" You see, belief in God and human dignity rise and fall together.

In the gospel above, there's more going on than meets the eye.

So, look at the gospel again. Of course Jesus cures a blind man named Bartimaeus. But did you notice to what Jesus gives credit for the cure? He said, "Go on your way, your faith has saved you." In other words, Bartimaeus' religious convictions — his belief in God, his faith — were critical in his cure. Jesus wanted Bartimaeus to know that his own health, his wholeness and his happiness depended on his relationship with God first and foremost. Without God he could not be healed.

The great psychologist Carl Jung said, "During the past 30 years, people from all civilized countries of the earth have consulted me. ... Among all my patients in the second half of their life (meaning older than 35) there has not been one whose problem in the last resort was not that of finding a religious outlook on life." In other words, religious belief contributes to good mental health. Belief in God and human wholeness rise and fall together.

One day, an atheist is spending a quiet day fishing when suddenly the Loch Ness Monster attacks his boat. In one easy flip, the beast tosses the man and boat a hundred feet in the air. It opens its mouth waiting to swallow him whole. The man cries out, "Oh, my God! Help me!" Suddenly the scene is frozen in time, and a booming voice says, "I thought you didn't believe in Me?" The atheist replies, "Come on, Lord, give me a break! A couple of seconds ago, I didn't believe in the Loch Ness Monster either!" God says, "Well, now that you're a believer you must understand I can't work a miracle just to save you from the jaws of the monster. But I can change hearts." The atheist thinks fast and says, "Ok, then have the Loch Ness Monster believe in you, too!" God says, "So be it." The scene is suddenly unfrozen, and as the man falls toward the beast, the monster folds his claws and prays, "Bless us, O Lord, and these thy gifts which we are about to receive through Christ, Our Lord. Amen." OK, maybe you'll like this one better: Now, they even have a Dial-a-Prayer for atheists. The phone rings and rings, but no one answers.

Folks, it is into this cultural war — of people of belief versus bah-humbug atheists, of faith versus disbelief — that Pope Benedict declared a "Year of Faith." In his Apostolic Letter, "Porta Fidei" (Door of Faith), he wrote, "It often happens that Christians are more concerned for the social, cultural and political consequences of their commitment, continuing to think of faith as a self-evident presupposition for life in society. In reality, not only can this presupposition no longer be taken for granted, but it is openly denied." The pope explains why, saying, "because a profound crisis of faith has affected many people." In other words, it's not as easy as that gas station attendant thought to bring people to faith. That teenage skateboarder was experiencing a "profound crisis of faith." And so too are many people you know personally. Atheism is rocking the roots of our society.

So, what should we do about it? Here are three suggestions. First, pray more. Pray God will give each of us the gift of faith, pray for those without faith, and memorize the Creed by heart. Second, be a witness to faith in public. Make the Sign of the Cross and say "Grace" before you bite into your Big Mac. People see that and remember there is a God. My mom has the beautiful custom of making the Sign of the Cross when she drives by a church. I always say a Hail Mary when I drive by a cemetery. I hope someday someone will say one for me! And third, stop, look and listen to life around you. Faith changes how we see everything. Can you imagine living life without God? How terrifying would the specter of death be if there were no afterlife or heaven? If there wasn't a God, why get out of bed in the morning? Joyce Kilmer captured life seen through faith in his popular poem, "Trees."

I think that I shall never see
A poem as lovely as a tree
A tree whose hungry mouth is prest
Against the earth's sweet flowing breast;

A tree that looks at God all day,
And lifts her leafy arms to pray;
A tree that may in Summer wear
A nest of robins in her hair;
Upon whose bosom snow has lain;
Who intimately lives with rain.
Poems are made by fools like me,
But only God can make a tree.

May I add a final line?
And only God makes you and me.

OUTSIDE DANGERS

Stepping outside your front door with great faith

•••

GENESIS 12:1-4A

The LORD said to Abram:

"Go forth from the land of your kinsfolk and from

your father's house to a land that I will show you.

"I will make of you a great nation, and I will bless you;

I will make your name great, so that you will be a blessing.

I will bless those who bless you and curse those who curse you.

All the communities of the earth shall find blessing in you."

Abram went as the LORD directed him.

One of my favorite childhood novels was *The Lord of the Rings* by J.R.R. Tolkien. It's about a humble little hobbit named Frodo and how his whole life changes with an ominous warning. His uncle Bilbo tells him: "It's a dangerous business, Frodo, going out your front door. You step onto the road and if you don't keep your feet, there's no knowing where you might be swept off to." Like a typical nephew, Frodo ignores his uncle's advice, steps out his front door, and is swept away on a wild adventure facing dragons, Dark Lords and certain death. Now, you should know that Frodo had every reason to stay put inside his home:

He was safe and comfortable, his world was predictable and he was respected by everyone, even a hometown celebrity. Life only begins, however, when we step out our front door into the wild world outside. In a very different book, and on a much larger stage, Shakespeare put these words on the lips of Brutus: "There is a tide in the affairs of men, which taken at the flood, leads on to fortune. Omitted, all the voyage of their life is bound in shallows and miseries." (*Julius Caesar*, IV, 3) Stepping out your front door is indeed dangerous; life is safer inside, but that life is also shallower. Outside lays greatness.

In the passage above, God invites Abram to step outside his front door, to take a step of faith. Listen to the famous call of Abram in Genesis 12 and see if you hear an echo of Bilbo's avuncular advice: "The Lord said to Abram, 'Go forth from the land of your kinsfolk and from your father's house to a land that I will show you.'" God sweetens the deal further by telling him that stepping away from safety also means stepping closer to greatness. The Lord continues, "I will make of you a great nation and I will bless you; I will make your name great, so that you will be a blessing." Abram took a great risk going out his front door — it would have been easier and safer to stay home in Ur of the Chaldeans — but that first step eventually led him to become the father of a great nation and, ultimately, the "Father of Faith." You see, it takes great faith to step out your front door.

I recently did a little going out my front door, too. What I found outside my front door was the wild world of social media. Believe me, it's a lot easier to fight orcs and trolls and Dark Lords than to survive the strange creatures crawling in cyberspace! I was visiting a family for supper, and their 13-year-old daughter set me up on Instagram. My name is "priestdude." I have a grand total of seven followers (all her friends). Someone else told me I should get a blog. Not knowing what that is, I said, "Eew! A blog sounds gooey and sticky — the blog!" Gross. You can access my blog at frjohnicchurch.blogspot.com. All this techno-geek stuff is not my cup of tea. I'm much more like a hobbit, who'd rather sip a real cup of tea in front of a blazing fire, reading a good book about Dark Lords and death-defying bravery. But if we never leave the safe haven of our homes, like Brutus said, "all our lives will be bound in shallows and miseries." I'm not exactly the "father of faith" like Abram, but I've learned that I can share the faith with thousands more through Facebook than I ever could face to face. The first step is always "the dangerous business of going out your front door."

God invites all of us to "go out our front door" and be swept off to an unknown future. It's like the bumper sticker that says, "If God is your co-pilot, switch places!" In other words, let God be your pilot (not you!) and let him fly you to places you never dreamed. Every Lent we participate in a sermon series with other Protestant pastors where we swap congregations. During one of these series, I stepped out of my comfort zone to preach at a local Presbyterian church. Have you ever visited a Protestant church and experienced their world of worship? It's a lot safer but also shallower to always stay put in your home church. If you're a Republican, I dare you to read Bill Clinton's speeches; they're quite good. If you're a "yellow-dog Democrat," pick up the pages of Ronald Reagan, the great communicator. (A yellow-dog Democrat will vote for a yellow dog before he votes for a Republican.) Many people never venture outside their political home — it's dangerous out there! I will forever be in awe of my parents who not only walked out their front door, but out of their home country to an unknown future. What great faith it takes to leave your family and friends, and especially Indian food, to start a new life: talk about being a father and mother of faith! My parents have never read Shakespeare, but they know better than Brutus that "there is a tide in the affairs of men, which taken at the flood leads on to fortune." We three children have inherited that fortune. Many husbands and wives fight and argue and sometimes divorce because neither one will step outside their front door, outside their own perspective, and see things from their spouse's point of view. That could be dangerous. How many parents and teenagers argue because neither wants to step foot into the other's wild world? If we choose safety, we also choose shallowness. It takes a lot of faith to step out your front door.

Bilbo wisely said: "It's a dangerous business, Frodo, going out your front door." Why is it dangerous? Because outside you will find orcs, and trolls and Dark Lords, Democrats and Presbyterians, Instagram and Twitter. But only if we step out that door will we begin the journey of faith, only then will we move over and let God be our pilot.

THE "BAD NEWS" OF BAPTISM
Living up to God's expectations for us

•••

LUKE 3:15-16, 21-22

The people were filled with expectation, and all were asking in
their hearts whether John might be the Christ. John answered
them all, saying, "I am baptizing you with water, but one mightier
than I is coming. I am not worthy to loosen the thongs of his
sandals. He will baptize you with the Holy Spirit and fire."
After all the people had been baptized and Jesus also had been
baptized and was praying, heaven was opened and the Holy
Spirit descended upon him in bodily form like a dove. And a
voice came from heaven, "You are my beloved Son; with
you I am well pleased."

The most moving baptism homily I've heard was delivered by a fellow
priest and close friend. It was so good, I can remember it word for word
15 years later! He started by quoting St. Francis of Assisi. He said, "St.
Francis of Assisi once said something very shocking. He said that if we
could see the soul of a newly baptized baby, we would be tempted to
bow down and worship." Then the priest gasped dramatically, obviously shocked at how we could be tempted to worship a mere human

being. With his audience fully intrigued, he continued, "Baptism creates an uncanny closeness between the soul and Christ, almost like that of twins. So that in seeing the newly baptized baby, you might almost think you're looking at Jesus himself! And that's why you'd be tempted to worship. Now, while the soul may look like Jesus, the body, eh, will only look like Bobby and Susie." Then Monsignor looked right at the baby's parents, and everyone laughed. Monsignor had made his point unforgettable: Baptism makes us like Jesus.

Author and theologian Archbishop Fulton Sheen once described the decisive difference that the grace of baptism makes. He said, "Grace divides the world into two kinds of people: the once born and the twice born. The once born are born only of their parents; the twice born are born of their parents and of God." He continued, "One group is what might be called natural. The other, in addition to having nature, share mysteriously in the divine life of God." Both Monsignor and Archbishop Sheen were articulating a fundamental mystery of our Catholic faith: Baptism makes us children of God; our souls bear a striking family resemblance to our older Brother, Jesus.

Jesus Himself was baptized in the Jordan River. But why did Jesus have to be baptized? After all, He was already the Son of God. Like so many things Jesus did — going off to pray, washing His disciples' feet — He was teaching by example. So, too, with baptism. But when we baptize a child, we are more than aping the Lord's example; something drastic happens to that baby. That child actually becomes adopted into the family of God. Having Jesus for a Brother means we can claim God as our Father. And that family relationship, by the way, is both good news and, in a sense, bad news. Why? Well, think about it this way: From whom do parents expect more: their own kids or the neighbor's kids? Obviously, they have higher standards for their own children. Parents love their children more than life itself, but they also expect their own children to be polite, do well in school, reach their full potential.

Parents always want their children to have more opportunities and to achieve greater goals than they reached themselves.

A college student wrote a letter home: "Dear folks, I feel miserable because I have to keep writing you for money. I feel ashamed and unhappy. I have to ask for another $100, but every cell in my body rebels. I beg on bended knee that you forgive me. Your son, Marvin." He added, "P.S. I felt so terrible I ran after the mailman who picked up this letter in the box at the corner. I wanted to take this letter and burn it. I prayed to God that I could get it back. But I was too late." A few days later he received a letter from his father. It said, "Your prayers were answered! Your letter never came!" Parents expect a lot more from their own kids, and they should.

Being baptized into God's family is both "good news" and "bad news." The good news is God loves us like His own children; the bad news is God loves us like His own children! God sets the bar high for His own children, just like good parents set high expectations for their own kids. Good parents constantly challenge their children with feedback like the following: "That's great honey, you made a B! Next time, see if you can make an A." "I'm proud of you for riding your bike with training wheels. Now, let's try it without them." "Well done, you're only playing five hours of video games a day! Let's cut that down to four!" HIGH expectations. These parental hopes and dreams are not limited to human parents, but also beat in the heart of our heavenly Father. God didn't just set the bar high for His firstborn Son, Jesus, but He does the same for all His sons and daughters reborn by baptism.

I hear some Catholics complain when the headlines report some scandal in the Catholic Church. They argue that the papers are too prone to pick on priests and the Catholic Church. But I disagree. In fact, I consider such coverage a compliment because it reinforces the fact that Christians in general, and church leaders in particular, are held to a higher standard. And that's a good thing because that standard is set not by the world, but by our Father, who expects a lot more from His children than from the neighbor's kids. That's why the Catholic Church, our Mother, sets sky high expectations for us, her children.

Recently, I visited an elderly lady in the hospital who had a breathing tube in her throat, making it impossible for her to talk. She was very, very sick. She used a notebook to write what she wanted to say. I gave her the anointing of the sick. And then I asked her for a favor. I asked, "Would you please pray for me? I believe the prayers of people who are suffering or hurting are very powerful. So, please offer those prayers and sacrifices for me." She nodded as tears rolled down her eyes and she squeezed my hand. That's something called "redemptive suffering," and I never miss a chance to cash in on it. Even your pains and problems count for God. God's children live by a higher standard, whether that child was born in Bethlehem or at the local hospital.

Do you know what children want more than anything? It's not more Legos. It's not backstage passes to a One Direction concert. It's not a $100 gift card to Forever 21 (whatever that is). No, what all children want is to hear their father and their mother say to them, "I am very proud of you." Jesus heard His Father say that at His baptism: "You are my beloved Son; with you I am well pleased." And nothing would give us more joy than to hear our heavenly Father say that to us. But that, my friends, is both good news and bad news.

THE ULTIMATE ANSWER
Solving problems through greater holiness

•••

MARK 9:30-37

They came to Capernaum and, once inside the house, Jesus
began to ask them, "What were you arguing about on the way?"
But they remained silent. They had been discussing among
themselves on the way who was the greatest. Then he sat down,
called the Twelve, and said to them, "If anyone wishes to be first,
he shall be the last of all and the servant of all."
Taking a child, he placed it in the their midst, and putting his
arms around it, he said to them, "Whoever receives one child
such as this in my name, receives me; and whoever receives me,
receives not me but the One who sent me."

If you've ever wondered what the ultimate answer is to life, the universe
and everything, it happens to be "42." At least, that was the answer
that Douglas Adams gave in his popular fiction book *The Hitchhiker's
Guide to the Galaxy.* The premise of the book is that a group of hyper-
intelligent, pan-dimensional beings want to learn "the answer to the
ultimate question of life, the universe and everything." So, they build a
supercomputer called "Deep Thought" specifically to find that answer.

It takes Deep Thought 7.5 million years to compute and check the answer, which turns out to be "42." It's a crazy great book if you're looking for one.

Now, people frequently ask me questions about all kinds of mysteries of life. Apparently, I look like a supercomputer like Deep Thought. And by the way, not once has the answer ever been "42." It's amazing the questions people ask me. Recently, a parishioner was having trouble with a tenant to whom she was renting her house. She wanted my advice. Really. Another parishioner was cheated by her boss at work and sought my counsel on what to do about it. Yet another asked me if I thought he should remain in town or relocate to get a better job in another state. Some younger parishioners ask my advice on dating. One young lady even introduced her boyfriend to me first, before she took him home to meet her parents. I guess she figured if he met "the Fr. John seal of approval," he might make it with the parents. A little word of advice: A celibate priest might not be your best bet for advice on your love life. As I listen to people, I wonder to myself, "Did I sleep through THAT many classes in seminary?" Surely they must have told us the answers to these questions. In any case, here's my answer to all the preceding questions: Be more holy. No matter how stifling the circumstances, regardless of how daunting the difficulties, or how convoluted the consequences may be, the right answer is always more holiness. In other words, the right answer is to be more patient and generous, maybe more cheerful or chaste, perhaps it's more forgiving or courageous, helpful or humble. You see, the answer to life's real questions is not "42." The answer is more holiness.

The book of Wisdom urges us to be just, even if the wicked try to destroy you. Being just is part of being holy. St. James enjoins his readers to be "pure, peaceable, gentle, compliant, full of mercy and good fruit, without being inconstant or insincere." In other words, be holy; all those are qualities of holiness. And Jesus, who is holiness Himself, says that His followers must be ready to suffer and be like little children and not seek to be great. Self-sacrifice and humility are two more characteristics of holiness. Jesus will summarize all His advice into one line in Matthew 5:48, saying, "Be holy as your heavenly Father is holy." You see, the Bible is the supercomputer God designed to answer all the difficulties and dilemmas that life deals us, and its one resounding answer is always "more holiness."

Once upon a time a chicken and a pig lived on a farm. The farmer was very good to them so they wanted to do something good for him. One day the chicken approached the pig and said, "I have a great idea! Let's make breakfast for the farmer." The pig said, "Sure, what shall we cook?" The chicken answered, "How about ham and eggs?" The pig shot back, "Hey, wait a minute! You're just making a contribution; I'm making a total commitment!" And that, too, is part of holiness: total commitment to Christ. Mahatma Gandhi once made this sobering statement about Christians: "If Christians would really live according to the teachings of Christ, as found in the Bible, all of India would be Christian today." Well, at least we got one Christian out of the bunch. But folks, one out of one billion ain't great. In other words, we don't have a lot of fully committed Christians; there are a lot more chickens than pigs.

What are the challenges, the questions, the doubts and dilemmas, the fears and foibles you face in life? Whatever they are, there is always one and only one answer: Be more holy. I once preached a sermon on humility and I mentioned political campaigns. Some people interpreted my homily as urging people to vote for the Republican candidate. But that's not true. I was urging them to be humble, which is part of holiness. How you vote should be an expression of humility rooted in truth. In other words, it's not voting Republican or Democrat that will save this country, but rather if your vote helps you to be more holy. This nation doesn't need more elephants or donkeys; it needs more pigs! It needs more saints. Be more holy. Maybe you are experiencing marriage problems. Our first instinct is to see all of the problems our spouse has: He drinks too much, she nags incessantly, he doesn't help around the house, she spends money frivolously. But the only solution to any marriage problem is for you — not your spouse — but for you to be more holy: more patient, more tolerant, more forgiving. Having trouble finding a date for Friday night? Forget e-harmony or match.com, be more holy. Don't know what to major in while in college or what career to choose? Be more holy. Can't figure out if God's calling you to be a priest or a nun? Be more holy. Can't decide how much to give in the weekly church offering? The answer is "42!" Everyone should give $42 every week. But you see, even if you're questioning how much to give in the collection on Sunday, the answer is be more holy. If you're trying to be holy, you'll know how much to give. I won't have to tell you.

Scott Hahn ended his book called *A Father Who Keeps His Promises* with this thought: "The crisis of the Church is not reducible to the lack of good catechesis, liturgies, theologians and so forth. It's a crisis of saints ... so, with Pope John Paul II, I urge you, "Make yourselves saints, and do so quickly!""

WITHOUT WAX

Living with sincerity and integrity

•••

MARK 7:1-8, 14-15, 21-23

When the Pharisees with some scribes who had come from
Jerusalem gathered around Jesus, they observed that some of
his disciples ate their meals with unclean — unwashed — hands.
Jews, including the Pharisees, do not eat without carefully
washing their hands, keeping the tradition of the elders.
And on coming from the marketplace they do not eat without
purifying themselves. And there are many other things that they
have traditionally observed, the purification of cups and jugs and
kettles and beds. So the Pharisees and scribes questioned him,
"Why do your disciples not follow the tradition of the elders
but instead eat a meal with unclean hands?" He responded,
"Well did Isaiah prophesy about you hypocrites, as it is written:
'This people honors me with their lips, but their hearts are far
from me; in vain do they worship me, teaching as doctrines
human precepts.' You disregard God's commandment but cling
to human tradition." He summoned the crowd again and said to
them, "Hear me, all of you, and understand. Nothing that enters
one from outside can defile that person; but the things that

come out from within are what defile. "From within people, from
their hearts, come evil thoughts, unchastity, theft, murder,
adultery, greed, malice, deceit, licentiousness, envy, blasphemy,
arrogance, folly. All these evils come from within and they defile."

Recently, I keep crossing paths with a character named Elie Wiesel. Elie is short for Eliezar, a name he shares with his grandfather. I first heard of him when a friend mentioned he was speaking at the Walton Arts Center in nearby Fayetteville, Ark. He addressed a capacity crowd of 1,200, and his speech was streamed live to 500 more gathered in the lobby because they couldn't get in. But I didn't bother to go. Then, a few weeks ago, I blessed a family's home and they gave me a book by Elie Wiesel called *Memoirs*, his autobiography. That's when I decided to find out who this guy was, and turns out he's no slouch. He's a professor at Boston University. He survived the Nazi concentration camp Auschwitz, won the Nobel Peace Prize in 1986, and received the Presidential Medal of Freedom, the U.S. Congressional Gold Medal and the French Legion of Honor, just for starters.

One thing that jumped out at me in *Memoirs* was the cunning of the Nazis. When they entered Wiesel's hometown of Sighet, Hungary, they were very polite and personable, almost dashing and debonair like the actors in *Mad Men*. Wiesel writes, "The Nazi officers made their own beds. They bowed politely to the ladies and kissed their hands like gentlemen. They offered candy to the children." But then Wiesel discovered their treachery: "Their courtesy was part of the plan conceived by Nazi Commander Adolf Eichmann. Their aim was to lull us into a false sense of security. Our confidence and credulity was their weapon." In other words, the Nazis used lies and deception to take the innocent and naïve Jews by the hand and lead them down the garden path right into the concentration camps. But what made the Nazis seem even more devious and diabolical was when they stood side by side with the goodness and even gullibility of the Jews. The contrast was stark: Adolf Eichmann or Elie Wiesel.

This two-faced duplicity is what Jesus is decrying in the gospel above. He quotes Isaiah, who said, "This people honors me with their lips, but their hearts are far from me." The Pharisees — who were NOT like Elie Wiesel — worried obsessively about appearances, like ritual cleanness, but their hearts were far from following God's law. But Jesus insists we have to be good all the way through, on the outside, on the inside and on every other side, too. We have to be good through and through.

A good friend and brother priest once explained the origin of the word "sincere." In the Middle Ages people would order marble furniture or sculptures. But some pieces of marble were chipped or cracked, and unscrupulous sculptors tried to hide those imperfections by filling in the gaps with wax, or in Latin "cera." Naturally, people wanted a guarantee that they bought 100 percent marble items, so they looked for the sign that said, "sine ceram," meaning "without wax." Jesus demands His followers also be "sine ceram" — sincere, authentic, not just honoring Jesus with their lips, but also with their hearts. Jesus' followers must never be duplicitous like the Nazis, but rather simple and sincere like Elie Wiesel.

Now, it can be very dangerous when we're careless with our words, like one of my parishioners found out recently. He is studying to be a deacon and he's excited. He was talking to a local Protestant preacher and, getting a little carried away, bought the man's horse. The preacher explained that the horse only understood two commands. He gallops forward when you say, "Thanks be to God," and he stops when you say, "Halleluiah." (After all, he's a preacher's horse, what do you expect?) Well, my parishioner took the horse for a ride and, full of the Holy Spirit, he kept saying "Thanks be to God! Thanks be to God!" which made the house run faster and faster. Suddenly, the horse and rider were headed toward a cliff, and he couldn't remember the word to make the horse stop (he's getting kind of old). He yelled, "Whoa, Nellie!" and "Stop!" and a few other things he yelled at the baseball players he used to coach. As the horse neared the cliff, he remembered the word and gasped, "Halleluiah!" The horse came to a screeching stop. Greatly relieved, he said, "Thanks be to God!" So, we all have to work on what we say, especially deacons in training.

Politics provides a fertile training ground for learning to exercise verbal discretion. Maybe you're tempted to sit back and criticize one party or another saying they're lying, exaggerating, or full of hot air, especially during election season. Instead, each of us should look closer at our own words and check our own sincerity. Do we say what we mean, and mean what we say? Are our words "sine ceram," truly sincere? Or, do we only "honor God with our lips but our hearts are far from Him?" Modern technology provides us with more avenues to be double-dealing and devious. Country artist Brad Paisley once sang "I'm so much cooler online." The song, titled *Online*, depicts a man with a totally different persona online than who he is in real life, one in which he's 6-feet-5-inches tall, has six-pack abs and drives a Mazaratti. Could this be one reason why so many young people spend time online, to be someone else, to be someone cooler? We can use Facebook, Twitter and social other media like so much "wax" to fill in the gaps in our own personalities and lives, instead of turning to Christ and letting Him help us be more "sine ceram," more authentic. Ohio State football coach Urban Meyer signed a "contract with his family" to put his family and his faith first, even over football. (Some of you might need to think about that.) But to help him keep his word, he wrote specific promises on a piece of paper and hung them in his office. Among his promises are: eat three meals a day, don't talk on the phone in church or at dinner, and watch his kids play sports. Meyer said it's the hardest contract he's ever signed. But that's being authentic through and through, not just paying lip service to fatherhood and faith.

It takes more than knowing when to say "Halleluiah" and "Thanks be to God" to ride a horse. And it takes more than that to be a good Christian.

WOE OR GIDDY-UP

Seeking joy rather than happiness

...

LUKE 3:10-14

The crowds asked John the Baptist, "What should we do?"
He said to them in reply, "Whoever has two cloaks should
share with the person who has none. And whoever has food
should do likewise."
Even tax collectors came to be baptized and they said to him,
"Teacher, what should we do?"
He answered them, "Stop collecting more than what
is prescribed."
Soldiers also asked him, "And what is it that we should do?"
He told them, "Do not practice extortion, do not falsely accuse
anyone, and be satisfied with your wages."

Would you rather be happy or joyful? Some may think, what's the difference? That's just two different ways of saying basically the same thing. But I disagree. In fact, I would go so far as to contend that not only is there a difference between the two, but they are almost the opposite of each other. I feel like that Harvard professor quizzing his new Ph.D. candidates to see if they were ready for his English Literature class. He asked a graduate from the University of Arkansas, "What is the opposite of pleasure?" The student said, "That would be pain." To the next student from the University of Oklahoma, he asked, "What is the opposite of depression?" He answered, "That is elation." To the third student from the University of Texas he asked, "And what is the opposite of woe?" The student replied, "Why, that'd be giddy-up!" So, you see, not all opposites are obvious, and that's the case with happiness and joy.

I learned how different joy and happiness are back in the eighth grade. That Christmas, for the first time in my life, I made straight A's on my report card. Now, you have to understand, I didn't really care about grades back then, probably because there wasn't a cool priest teaching us Latin, as I did at St. Joseph. So, those A's were not for me, but more like a Christmas gift for my parents. I still remember how pleased they were. That same Christmas I received a bike as a gift from them. It was a fast bike, the fastest in the neighborhood, and I even named it "Flash." Those two experiences made me feel very different. Receiving that bike made me happy, which lasted a while but eventually evaporated. Giving that report card to my parents, on the other hand, gave me immense joy. Joy was deep, it lasted a long time, I still feel it today, and I wanted more of it! That's the difference between happiness and joy. Happiness is the pleasure of receiving something, short-lived; joy is the pleasure of giving something, enduring. That's why Acts 20:35 says, "It is more blessed to give than to receive." In other words, joy is not only greater than happiness; it is almost its opposite.

The third Sunday of Advent is called "Gaudate Sunday" and priests with more moxie than me even wear rose-colored vestments. "Gaudate" means "Rejoice!" and so some call today "Joy Sunday." But notice we don't call today "Happiness Sunday," as if we're excited about getting a bike for Christmas in two weeks. No, this is "Joy Sunday" because Christmas is about the pleasure of giving. The people in Luke's gospel above caught this difference. When John preaches to the crowds, the soldiers and the tax collectors, they ask, "What must we do?" And John tells them: Stop collecting excessive taxes, give to the poor, treat your soldiers with respect. In other words, experience the lasting joy of giving, and stop chasing the flimsy happiness of receiving. This is how you prepare for the coming of Christ, who has come to give Himself to us and teach us how to do the same.

I worry that our country is seeking more and more happiness — what we can get for ourselves — and less and less joy — how we can give to others. During modern-day presidential debates, neither candidate would dare repeat those famous lines from John F. Kennedy's inaugural address: "And so my fellow Americans, ask not, what your country can do for you, ask what you can do for your country." That would have spelled political suicide because who would vote for someone who asks us to make sacrifices? Today, sadly, my fellow Americans only want to know, "What can my country do for me?" But the Christ Child teaches us it is more blessed to give than to receive. I'll never forget what the late, beloved principal of Catholic High School in Little Rock, Ark., Fr. George Tribou, told us Catholic High boys about attending Mass. He said, "I hear boys complaining these days that they don't get anything out of the Mass. Well, let me tell you boys something: You don't come to Mass to get something out of it. You come to Mass to give something — to give some of your time, to give some of your attention, to give some of your love." Those words worked a kind of Copernican revolution in my mind: I had the wrong thing at the center of my universe, me instead of Jesus. I was more focused on getting instead of giving. By twelfth grade in high school I had forgotten the lessons learned back in eighth grade, like the joy of giving a report card with straight A's to my parents. Fr. Tribou, like John the Baptist, taught me once again the difference between happiness and joy.

Some years ago, I asked my parents what they would like for

Christmas. They replied, "Son, there is only one thing we want. We would really like our three children to love each other, to stop fighting and not argue all the time." I said, "OK, well, what else would you like, because that's not going to happen." But like so many first-generation immigrants, my parents learned early on the joy that comes from living for your children, instead of living for yourself. I often receive direct donations from parishioners who say, "Father, this is for the church, use it as you deem best. We don't want anyone to know where it came from." See, they get it. There's a difference between happiness and joy; in fact, they are almost polar opposites. And a lot of other parishioners get it, too, those who give generously of their time and talents, even if they don't have a lot of money. They wonder like the people in the gospel, "And what must we do?"

People often ask, "What would Fr. John like for Christmas?" What I would really like is for my parishioners to be at peace, for husbands and wives not to fight and argue, for parents and teenagers to be more understanding, for sibling rivalry to cease, that we all forgive and forget past hurts. And I'd really like my parents to stop arguing and fighting. Yeah, I'm probably not going to get that, am I? But I hope you've learned the difference between joy and happiness, a lesson we must learn again and again. They are as different as "Woe" and "Giddy-up!"

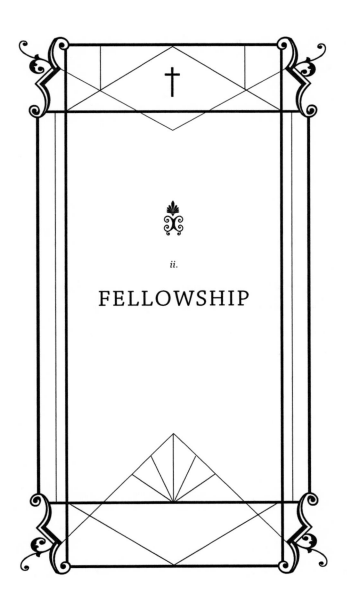

ii.

FELLOWSHIP

My favorite prose work by seventeenth century poet, satirist and cleric John Donne is *Meditation 17*, in which he waxes eloquently about the unbreakable bond between people. He asserts: "No man is an island, entire of itself; every man is a piece of the continent, a part of the main." Then Donne employs this startling image, saying, "If a clod be washed away by the sea, Europe is the less." What happens to another person, regardless of how far she lives or how unfamiliar she might be, mysteriously affects me. And what happens to me, in turn, touches her. Reverend Martin Luther King, Jr. echoed this same sentiment when he spoke to the graduates of Oberlin College: "What we are facing today is the fact that, through our scientific and technological genius, we've made of this world a neighborhood. And now, through our moral and ethical commitment, we must make of it a brotherhood. We must all learn to live together as brothers; or we will perish together as fools. This is the great issue facing us today. No individual can live alone; no nation can live alone. We are tied together." Not surprisingly, King goes on to quote Donne's famous line from *Meditation 17*. What Donne and King both perceived was that what unites people is far deeper and stronger than what divides us; that unity should be protected and promoted.

St. Paul realized that a similar but far deeper unity exists among the members of the Church, and in 1 Corinthians 12, described the community of Christians as "the body of Christ." Paul instructs the Corinthians saying, "Just as a body, though one, has many parts, but all the parts form one body, so it is with Christ. ... Now you are the body of Christ, and each one of you is a part of it" (1 Corinthians 12:12, 27). That is, humanity's oneness is not based on some vague sense of camaraderie, but rather, on something very solid and strong: the person of Jesus. Because we belong to Jesus, we belong to each other.

That common bond in Christ underlies every homily in this chapter. Among the topics touched upon here, you'll find loving the unlovable, the great value of simple kindness, the urgent need to work for communion and overcome division, loving the poor as our masters, and never giving up on each other. We love others because we first love Christ; each person is part of His body. It's hard to imagine how the immense continent of Europe would be diminished if a tiny clod of earth were washed into the sea, but so it is, if you have the eyes to see the ties that bind together the human family. How much more, then, should we foster genuine and heartfelt Christian fellowship; a brother or sister in Christ is worth infinitely more than a tiny clod of earth, if only we have the eyes of faith to see how we all belong to the Body of Christ.

CROOKED LINES OF CHRISTMAS

Loving the unlovable members of our families

...

MATTHEW 1:1-16

The book of the genealogy of Jesus Christ, the son of David, the son of Abraham. Abraham became the father of Isaac, Isaac the father of Jacob, Jacob the father of Judah and his brothers. Judah became the father of Perez and Zerah, whose mother was Tamar. Perez became the father of Hezron, Hezron the father of Ram, Ram the father of Amminadab.

Amminadab became the father of Nahshon, Nahshon the father of Salmon, Salmon the father of Boaz, whose mother was Rahab. Boaz became the father of Obed, whose mother was Ruth. Obed became the father of Jesse, Jesse the father of David the king. David became the father of Solomon, whose mother had been the wife of Uriah. Solomon became the father of Rehoboam, Rehoboam the father of Abijah, Abijah the father of Asaph. Asaph became the father of Jehoshaphat, Jehoshaphat the father of Joram, Joram the father of Uzziah. Uzziah became the father of Jotham, Jotham the father of Ahaz, Ahaz the father of Hezekiah. Hezekiah became the father of Manasseh,

Manasseh the father of Amos, Amos the father of Josiah.
Josiah became the father of Jechoniah and his brothers at
the time of the Babylonian exile. After the Babylonian exile,
Jechoniah became the father of Shealtiel, Shealtiel the father of
Zerubbabel, Zerubbabel the father of Abiud.
Abiud became the father of Eliakim, Eliakim the father of Azor,
Azor the father of Zadok. Zadok became the father of Achim,
Achim the father of Eliud, Eliud the father of Eleazar.
Eleazar became the father of Matthan, Matthan the father of
Jacob, Jacob the father of Joseph, the husband of Mary. Of her
was born Jesus who is called the Christ.

I did something this Christmas I've never done before. I read every word of every Christmas letter that I received in the mail. Yes, this is the first time I did that. I hope I don't offend any of my friends or parishioners by revealing this: I really do love to hear from them and catch up on the "year in review" of their families. My favorite letter this year had two parts. The top of the letter began with a brief paragraph of three lines called an "Executive Summary," hitting the highlights, and the rest of the letter dove into the delightful details.

The letters ranged from the comical to the tragic, from the sarcastic to the sentimental. People recounted with gratitude the blessings like the birth of new babies and weddings they celebrated or attended. They mourned the loss of loved ones who passed away this year. And they rejoiced to see children and grandchildren flower into young adults who achieved awards and chose careers. But there was one thing conspicuously missing from every Christmas letter: There was no mention of the "black sheep" of the family. You know who I'm talking about: that family member every family has but no one talks about — the uncle who drinks too much, the sister who has left the Church and doesn't go to any church, the brother who was imprisoned for selling drugs, a sibling who left the family because of a fight and hasn't been heard from since. It reminds me of that farcical Christmas song "Grandma got run over by a reindeer, walking home from our house Christmas Eve." But do you remember why she got run over? "She'd been drinking too much eggnog, and we begged her not to go. But she'd left her medication, so she stumbled out the door into the snow." We'd all like to plan and pull off the Norman Rockwell Christmas gathering, but the fact of the matter is most of our families are not only full of in-laws, but also a good number of out-laws. And we shouldn't forget about the out-laws at Christmas.

The gospel passage above is one of my favorites of the whole Bible, and the one most priests and deacons dread to read. It's the glorious genealogy of Jesus, going all the way back to Abraham, the father of our faith. Now, most people perspire over pronouncing the names properly and just want to get the reading over with. But when they do, they miss who these ancestors really were. Of course, you have the Hall of Famers of Jesus' lineage, like the patriarchs Abraham, Isaac and Jacob, the kings David, Solomon and Josiah, and of course, St. Joseph. But mixed in are also some unsavory characters, some "out-laws" according to Jewish tradition, like Rahab who was a harlot. There was Ruth, a Moabite who was not part of the chosen people. And who can forget Uriah, the murdered husband of Bathsheba, with whom King David had an affair? In a sense, you can read the genealogy like St. Matthew's Christmas letter to us. He hits the highlights of "the glory days," the Who's Who of the genealogical lineup, recounting the miraculous births and the high achievements. But there's a notable difference between Matthew's letter and ours: He's not afraid to acknowledge the black sheep of Jesus' family. Why? Because Matthew sees that God's plan of salvation is so wise and so good it flows flawlessly through the out-laws as well as the in-laws, through the sinners as well as the saints, through the black sheep all the way down the annals of history to the spotless Lamb. It is often said that "God can write straight with crooked lines." Well, there's no better proof of that straight path made up of crooked lines than Jesus' own genealogy. Matthew didn't forget to mention the out-laws in his Christmas letter.

This past summer, I watched the movie "Cars 2" with my nieces and nephews. The most important scene of the movie didn't have anything to do with car racing, but everything to do with a tow truck named Mater. Two British secret agents want to fit Mater with a disguise so he can go undercover. Agent Holley Shiftwell explains the computer has to buff out and repair Mater's scratches and dents in order to apply the disguise properly. Mater replies, "Well then, no thank ye. I don't get them dents buffed, pulled, filled or painted by nobody. They way too valuable." A surprised Holley asks, "Your dents are valuable? Really?" Mater explains, "I come by each one with my best friend, Lightning McQueen. I don't fix these. I want to remember these dents forever." For as slow and simple as Mater seemed, he was smart enough to know that "dents are valuable," and not only do you not fix them, you also learn to cherish them. Mater, like Matthew, would have included everyone in his Christmas letter, the in-laws as well as the out-laws; you don't buff out the dents.

Christmas is a time of family gatherings, time-honored traditions, fun and frolic, love and laughter. But it can also be teeming with tension and fraught with memories of unforgiven faults. We might start to embrace that old sentiment, "The only thing better than seeing family come, is seeing family go." Or, as Benjamin Franklin famously remarked, "Guests are like fish, they both begin to smell after three days." So, during the holidays — the holy days — when your patience and peace have evaporated, when your sympathy and smile have withered like the garland on your porch, think of the crooked lines of Christmas. God's plan of salvation embraced Rahab, Ruth and Uriah; we wouldn't have Jesus without them. Cherish your family like Mater cherished his dents, instead of wanting them to be "buffed, pulled, filled or painted." And if there are family or friends you've ignored, Christmas is the perfect time to reach out to those "crooked lines in your life."

There's a mysterious little line we sing at Easter that touches the same chord. The Exultet declares, "Oh happy fault, that earned so great, so glorious a Redeemer." In other words, it was thanks to the very first out-law of the human race, Adam, that Jesus came to save us. Do you remember how that song about Grandma and the reindeer ends? It goes, "Grandma got run over by a reindeer, walking home from our house Christmas Eve. You can say there's no such thing as Santa, but as for me and Grandpa we believe." It took Grandma's stumbling stupor in the snow to bring Grandpa and Junior to believe in Santa. Maybe it's the out-laws we leave out of our Christmas letters who will help us to believe in a Savior.

KINDNESS IN A CUP

Showing kindness as the hallmark of our Christianity

•••

MATTHEW 13:24-33

Jesus proposed another parable to the crowds, saying:

"The kingdom of heaven may be likened to a man

who sowed good seed in his field.

While everyone was asleep his enemy came

and sowed weeds all through the wheat, and then went off.

When the crop grew and bore fruit, the weeds appeared as well.

The slaves of the householder came to him and said,

'Master, did you not sow good seed in your field?

Where have the weeds come from?'

He answered, 'An enemy has done this.'

His slaves said to him, 'Do you want us to go and pull them up?'

He replied, 'No, if you pull up the weeds you might uproot the

wheat along with them. Let them grow together until harvest;

then at harvest time I will say to the harvesters,

First collect the weeds and tie them in bundles for burning;

but gather the wheat into my barn.'"

He proposed another parable to them.

"The kingdom of heaven is like a mustard seed that a person

> took and sowed in a field. It is the smallest of all the seeds,
> yet when full-grown it is the largest of plants.
> It becomes a large bush, and the 'birds of the sky
> come and dwell in its branches.'"
> He spoke to them another parable.
> "The kingdom of heaven is like yeast that a woman took and
> mixed with three measures of wheat flour
> until the whole batch was leavened."

In the seminary, I learned all the usual do's and don'ts about being a priest, but I also learned some surprising stuff. I'll never forget when one professor revealed to me the one sin a priest can commit that his parishioners will never forgive. They'll forgive him if his homilies are long, meandering and pointless. They'll forgive him if he struggles with drinking or drugs or depression. They'll be understanding if he asks too frequently for money or picks too much on the deacon. They'll forgive all these things and much more. But the one thing they'll never forgive him for is a lack of kindness, not being compassionate and failing to be caring. When your mom is in the hospital, when you lose your job, when you get a divorce and you turn to talk to the priest, you expect empathy and understanding. And if we priests fail in that crucial moment, then we usually lose that person for good. Do you know of anyone who has left the Church because of an unkind word by a priest? One of the things I remember most fondly about Fr. Correnti, my former mentor and brother priest, was his soft smile and his listening ear. I could tell him anything. He was kind to a fault. Pastor and leadership guru John Maxwell summarized this leadership trait well when he said, "People don't care how much you know, until they know how much you care." Caring, compassion, kindness should be the defining quality of every priest. People will forgive you if you lack everything else, but not if you lack kindness.

In the gospel above, Jesus describes the Kingdom of God using parables. But did you notice how in each parable the distinguishing quality of the Kingdom is kindness? Just think about it. The first parable concerns the weeds and the wheat. The farmer kindly allows the weeds to grow with the wheat until the harvest. The second parable is about the mustard seed that grows into a huge bush, kindly welcoming all the birds of the sky, without preference or prejudice. In the third parable, the yeast kindly reaches every corner of the mass of dough, helping it all to rise. Now, this is not to say that the Kingdom of God is spineless or mamby-pamby, just going along to get along, just Mr. Nice Guy. Jesus warns that the Day of Judgment is coming like a freight train, when the weeds will be separated from the wheat and flung into the fire. But until that final day, the Kingdom should be kind and not cruel. You see, people will forgive everything except unkindness in a priest. Why? Because people instinctively know that kindness should be the characteristic quality of the Kingdom of God, as well.

I recently heard of one act of kindness that backfired. Are you familiar with this hilarious story circulating on the internet? We all know how daddies dote on their daughters. A lady wrote: "One day, my mother was out and my dad was in charge of me. I was maybe 2½ years old. Someone had given me a little tea set as a gift, and it was one of my favorite toys. Daddy was in the living room engrossed in the evening news, when I brought him a little cup of tea, which was just water. After several cups of tea and lots of praise for such yummy tea, my mom came home. My dad made her wait in the living room to watch me bring him a cup of tea, because it was just the cutest thing! Mom waited, and sure enough, here I came down the hall with the cup of tea for Daddy, and she watched him drink it all up. Then she said, as only a mother would, "Did it ever occur to you that the only place she can reach to get water is the toilet?" So, kindness can come at a pretty high cost. But it's always worth it.

Does kindness characterize your Christianity? Because if it doesn't, it should. When was the last time you did something that was unsolicited, surprising and spontaneously kind? I recall a time when I drove through McDonald's to pick up a Big Mac. A teen greeted me at the window and said, "No priest pays for a Big Mac in this McDonald's!" (By the way, I'd like to eat at the local four-star restaurant next week, in case someone is looking for an act of kindness.) Consider this stunning act of kindness: When New York Yankees shortstop Derek Jeter crushed his 3,000th hit at Yankee Stadium, it was a homerun, and that ball was easily worth millions of dollars. But the fan who got the ball, Christian Lopez, did a shocking thing. He just returned the ball to Jeter. "It wasn't about the money," he said. "It was about a milestone and I wasn't going to take that away from him. Mr. Jeter deserved it. It's all his." Would you have committed such an outlandish act of kindness? Psychologists say that in raising children, you should praise them 10 times for one every time you correct them. In the same way, compliments rather than criticism should leap from every Christian's lips. And don't wait for someone else to be kind to you first — beat them to it. Smile at the crabby cashier at the corner gas station, and wish them a blessed day. Pray a Hail Mary for the people who cut you off in traffic. Perform an act of kindness for your spouse when they least expect it, and when you think they least deserve it. One parishioner always ends our conversations with the question, "Father, is there anything I can do for you?" I always answer, "Pray for me." But that man embodies the key quality of the Kingdom: kindness. Romans 12:10 reminds us, "Outdo one another in showing kindness." In other words, be kind to a fault.

Being a good Christian is not terribly complicated, and it's not too costly either. It can be as simple as a smile or as humble as a hug. And please pray for us priests, that kindness will be the one quality we are never short on. Oh, and by the way: If I ever come over to your house, please tell you children that I don't drink tea; only bottled water.

LONG SPOON OF LOVE

Serving in heaven rather than reigning in hell

•••

MATTHEW 20:1-16A

Jesus told his disciples this parable:

"The kingdom of heaven is like a landowner

who went out at dawn to hire laborers for his vineyard.

After agreeing with them for the usual daily wage,

he sent them into his vineyard.

Going out about nine o'clock,

the landowner saw others standing idle in the marketplace,

and he said to them, 'You too go into my vineyard,

and I will give you what is just.' So they went off.

And he went out again around noon,

and around three o'clock, and did likewise.

Going out about five o'clock,

the landowner found others standing around,

and said to them, 'Why do you stand here idle all day?'

They answered, 'Because no one has hired us.'

He said to them, 'You too go into my vineyard.'

When it was evening the owner of the vineyard

said to his foreman,

'Summon the laborers and give them their pay,

beginning with the last and ending with the first.'

When those who had started about five o'clock came,

each received the usual daily wage.

So when the first came, they thought that they would receive

more, but each of them also got the usual wage.

And on receiving it they grumbled against the landowner, saying,

'These last ones worked only one hour, and you have made them

equal to us, who bore the day's burden and the heat.'

He said to one of them in reply,

'My friend, I am not cheating you.

Did you not agree with me for the usual daily wage?

Take what is yours and go.

What if I wish to give this last one the same as you?

Or am I not free to do as I wish with my own money?

Are you envious because I am generous?'

Thus, the last will be first, and the first will be last."

Many years ago I heard a talk by the theologian Dr. Scott Hahn that rocked my world. Be forewarned: This isn't typical cocktail party conversation, but it completely changed how I look at the world, including how I look at cocktail parties! Hahn explained why the angels, especially Lucifer, chose to sin against God and ended up in hell. You see, angels are beings of brilliant beauty, light and logic — the highest of all creation. They understand all reality in a neatly organized, hierarchical order: At the top you have God, then below Him the angels, then comes man, then animals, then plants, followed by minerals and so on. The different levels relate to one another in a very reasonable and logical way, too: The lower level always serves the higher level. So, animals serve people, people in turn serve the angels and the angels serve God. (By the way, this description eerily echoed Ayn Rand's *Atlas Shrugged*, a book about a world in which the lesser serves the greater. The book was wildly popular, but also wildly mistaken, leaving no room for religion or charity. Atlas might have "shrugged," but that book made me shudder.) Hahn went on to explain that God tested Lucifer by requiring him to flip-flop his own logic and instead of man serving the angels, the angels would have to serve human beings. How did Lucifer reply? He not only said, "No," but "Hell no!" (It's OK if a priest says "hell.") And hell is exactly where Lucifer — now turned Satan — went. You see, God was really inviting Lucifer into the heart of the Holy Trinity, but the logic that unlocks that Divine Door of heaven is not the earthly logic of master-slave, but a heavenly "theo-logic," or the logic of God, where the greater serves the lesser. Milton, in *Paradise Lost*, put these famous words in Satan's mouth: "I would rather reign in hell than serve in heaven." That defines the difference between heaven and hell. In heaven you happily serve others, especially those who are lower or lesser or weaker than you, but in hell you miserably make others who are weaker mind you.

One day an angel took a man to see heaven and hell. In hell, the man noticed a long, narrow banquet table with people seated on both sides facing each other. The table was filled with sumptuous food and drink but with extremely long forks and spoons. The people in hell were starving because they couldn't get the food to their own mouths. Then the angel took him to heaven, where he saw exactly the same sight: a long narrow table, again decked with divine delicacies, but with one difference. In heaven, the people fed those on the other side of the table with the long spoons, not themselves. It is obviously better to serve in heaven than to reign in hell.

In the gospel above, Jesus teaches this theo-logic of heaven to His disciples in a parable. Jesus paints a paradoxical picture in which those who work less actually get paid as much as those who work more. Ayn Rand would have shrugged if she had heard this parable! But the point of the parable is not the workers, but rather the generosity of the owner. Jesus wants His disciples to emulate the owner's example: the greater serving the lesser, the rich helping the poor, the strong taking care of the weak. And He drives home His point by saying: "Thus the last shall be first and the first shall be last." In other words, it's better to serve in heaven than to reign in hell.

People should see us Catholics serving those around us too, but sometimes they see other inspiring things. One day, Sr. Margaret Mary was out making her rounds when she ran out of gas. Fortunately, there was a gas station only a block away, so she walked to the station to borrow a can of gas. The attendant told her the only gas can was loaned out, but if she could wait, he'd run out and get her one. Sister was in a hurry, so she walked back to the car, noticed the bedpan that she was carrying to a patient, and returned to the gas station to fill the bedpan up with gas. As she was pouring the gas into the car, two men were watching from across the street. One of them turned to the other and said, "If it starts, I'm turning Catholic." So, we can inspire people with lots of things, but the best way is by serving others.

My friends, are you learning the language of heaven or the logic of hell? Are you serving others or serving yourself? Apparently, even billionaires are learning to serve others. Bill Gates and Warren Buffett started "The Giving Pledge" initiative, calling billionaires to donate half of their fortunes to charity before they die or leave it in their wills. Does anyone know any of those billionaires? Please put in a good word for your church! But those people are starting to feed the people seated across the table at the heavenly banquet. You don't have to be a billionaire to serve others. When I was at St. Joseph, members of my own church did so through our refugee resettlement program and our Honduras mission effort. And thanks to the generosity of our congregation, our school started an "Adopt-A-Student Program," helping one deserving student pay for his or her tuition for one year. Can you provide that help to a child? Are there ways you can volunteer your time, your money, your treasures at your own local charities?

Let me make one thing clear: This message is not so much for you who already give so graciously, but rather for those who find it so hard to give to others because they focus fiercely on themselves. You know, that 80 percent of the Pareto Principle, who only give 20 percent of the effort. I'm telling you the truth: The only way to reserve a seat at the heavenly banquet is if you learn to feed others with the long spoon of love; otherwise, you will sit and starve, staring at the cold logic of Lucifer in hell.

So, did this homily rock your world as much as Scott Hahn's talk rocked mine? It's OK if it didn't. But at least believe me more than Satan. It is better to serve in heaven than to reign in hell.

NEVER GIVE UP

Waiting patiently as the Spirit works on us

...

MATTHEW 21:28-32

Jesus said to the chief priests and elders of the people:

"What is your opinion? A man had two sons.

He came to the first and said,

'Son, go out and work in the vineyard today.'

He said in reply, 'I will not,' but afterwards changed

his mind and went.

The man came to the other son and gave the same order.

He said in reply, 'Yes, sir,' but did not go.

Which of the two did his father's will?"

They answered, "The first."

Jesus said to them, "Amen, I say to you, tax collectors

and prostitutes are entering the kingdom of God before you.

When John came to you in the way of righteousness,

you did not believe him;

but tax collectors and prostitutes did.

Yet even when you saw that, you did not later change

your minds and believe him."

One of the most rewarding things to do as a priest, as well as one of the most frustrating, is preaching at Mass. It's rewarding when people tell you your words made them think or touched their lives. But it's frustrating when they can't remember a word you said five minutes after you're done. I take consolation in knowing that even in the "ho-hum homilies" I've delivered, I still plant a seed that the Holy Spirit can make sprout later.

Now, some preachers go to great lengths to make their point, so people don't forget. A while back one of our deacons used a visual demonstration to drive home his message. He wanted to emphasize the dangers of drinking alcohol, smoking cigarettes and eating too much chocolate. So, at the beginning of his homily, he brought out four jars and put a worm in each jar. The first worm went into a jar full of alcohol, the second into a jar filled with cigarette smoke, the third worm into a jar of chocolate syrup, and the fourth worm was placed into a jar of good, clean soil. At the end of his homily, the deacon reported the results: the worm in the jar of alcohol was dead, the worm in the jar of cigarette smoke was dead; the worm in the jar of chocolate syrup was also dead. The worm in the jar of clean soil was alive and well. The deacon asked the people what they learned. An old woman sitting in the back raised her hand and said, "As long as you drink, smoke and eat chocolate, you won't get worms!" That pretty much ended the sermon. But every preacher knows that no matter what someone's reaction may be, our words are like small seeds planted in the heart that the Spirit can make sprout. Preachers never give up on people.

In the gospel above, Jesus tells the parable of a father who never gives up on his sons. A man commands two sons to work in his vineyard: One says "no" but later changes his mind and goes anyway. The second says, "Sure!" but in the end, he ignores the father's request. Notice that even though the first son eventually obeyed, it took time. His reply was "no" at first. You see, it takes time for the Holy Spirit to make the father's words sprout in the heart of the young man. Jesus teaches that wise parents are not discouraged by the denials of their defiant children; instead they patiently persist, knowing the Spirit is on their side. Parents, like preachers, don't give up on people.

I just finished reading the autobiography of Supreme Court Justice Clarence Thomas, entitled, *My Grandfather's Son*. The curious title comes from the fact that when he was 7 years old, Clarence Thomas went to live with his grandparents. Thomas attributes his determination, his devotion and especially his discipline to the lessons he learned from his grandfather, whom he called "Daddy." Here's an example of how Daddy, who was very tough, raised him. Thomas and his brother, Myers, were never allowed to miss school, no matter how severe the circumstances. To make his message memorable, Daddy added, "And if you die, I'm going to drag your dead bodies to school and leave them there for three days. Just in case you're faking!" The boys knew Daddy would do exactly that, too. At the end of the book, Thomas confesses his debt to his grandparents: "Daddy and Aunt Tina taught me all they knew and gave me all they had: their wisdom, their energy, their way of life. For a long while I had, like the prodigal son, abandoned them and what they had taught me. Finally, I had returned to their ways, vowing to live my life as a memorial to theirs." You know, Thomas wrote this book in 2007; but it took 40 years for those seeds planted during his boyhood to sprout into a garden of goodness. Just like the son in the parable, Clarence Thomas also said, "No" at first, but later in life said, "Yes." Thomas' grandfather never gave up on him.

Have you ever given up on someone? Have you ever felt so frustrated and infuriated with someone's stubbornness or selfishness that you said, "Ah, what's the use! He's never going to change! She'll always be the same!"? Well, don't give up on people. You have the Spirit on your side, and the Spirit is still nurturing those seeds. A priest friend of mine working in the Bronx never gives up. He once famously said,

"I pray every day that the singer Madonna will change her life, make a sincere confession and become a cloistered Carmelite nun." Hey, if you're going to pray, pray big!

The Catholic Church stands against the death penalty for one fundamental reason: We don't give up on people. Give the Holy Spirit time to work. Why? Because He's not done with us yet. Don't give up on your spouse. Don't give up on your children. Don't give up on your parents. Don't give up on your neighbor. And whatever you do, never, ever give up on your priest! Don't give up on other people, because someday, you may need others not to give up on you.

I heard Clarence Thomas speak several years ago in Little Rock, Ark., after the Red Mass, which is offered for those in the legal profession. His testimony was very personal and very moving. He mentioned something he had omitted in his autobiography. Growing up in Savannah, Ga., he had been an altar server to then-Msgr. Andrew McDonald, who would later become bishop of Little Rock, Ark. It was at Bishop McDonald's request that Justice Thomas came to speak to us. I'm sure Msgr. McDonald preached many sermons to Clarence Thomas during his youth, some soul-stirring, others soporific. But whatever he said, he planted seeds that would sprout into a garden of grace through the power of the Holy Spirit. Through most of his adult life, Thomas had been away from the Catholic Church. But in the mid-1990s he returned to the Church and is a practicing Catholic today. Bishops don't give up on people.

Let's make a deal: I won't give up on you; and you don't give up on me. Deal?

NO MAN IS AN ISLAND

Cherishing our common bond with others

•••

LUKE 9:28B-36

Jesus took Peter, John, and James and

went up a mountain to pray.

While he was praying his face changed in appearance

and his clothing became dazzling white.

And behold, two men were conversing with him,

Moses and Elijah, who appeared in glory

and spoke of his exodus that he was going

to accomplish in Jerusalem.

Peter and his companions had been overcome by sleep,

but becoming fully awake,

they saw his glory and the two men standing with him.

As they were about to part from him, Peter said to Jesus,

"Master, it is good that we are here;

let us make three tents, one for you, one for Moses,

and one for Elijah."

But he did not know what he was saying.

While he was still speaking,

a cloud came and cast a shadow over them,

and they became frightened when they entered the cloud.

Then from the cloud came a voice that said,

"This is my chosen Son; listen to him."

After the voice had spoken, Jesus was found alone.

They fell silent and did not at that time tell anyone

what they had seen.

Everyone has noticed how geese fly in the shape of the letter "V." But do you know why they have this curious custom? The goose at the tip of the "V" takes the brunt of the wind-resistance. The two geese a little behind him have to endure less wind, and the resistance gets gradually less and less, until the last two geese, at the very tips of the V, are basically on cruise control, not working at all. When the lead goose gets tired, he flies back to the last spot and relaxes, while another takes the lead position. By the way, do you know that a group of geese is called a "gaggle"? That reminds me of what Bishop Sartain, a colleague and friend, said when he was moved to Joliet, Ill. He was poking fun of being from the South and asked the congregation, "You know that in the South we say, 'ya'll.' But do you know what the plural of 'ya'll' is?" Everyone looked bewildered. The Bishop smiled and said, "It's 'all-a-ya'll.'" Here's something else interesting about how geese fly: They honk at each other. Why? Well, that's really a honk of encouragement for the goose at the front. I'm not joking! Hearing the honking from behind, the lead goose is inspired to work hard and push the group forward, not only because soon he'll be relaxing at the end of the line, but also because he hears the encouragement from his friends. President Lyndon Johnson, to rally the country together, once said: "There are no problems we cannot solve together, and very few that we can solve by ourselves." You see, human beings, like geese, can fly so much farther, and accomplish so much more, when we work together than we ever could going it alone.

In the gospel above, we see that Jesus also needs the encouragement of others to fulfill His great mission. The gospel scene is Mt. Tabor, and Jesus is transfigured before His closest disciples, Peter, James and John. But what's even more interesting are the two men who appear on either side of Jesus on the mountain: Moses and Elijah. What are Moses and Elijah doing there? Luke tells us, "They spoke of the exodus that [Jesus] was going to accomplish in Jerusalem." In other words, Moses and Elijah, who had themselves suffered and been victorious in the Old Testament, were now encouraging Jesus as He was about to face His own great test. You might say they were like those "honking geese" cheering for Jesus to carry on.

You know, if you think about it, this gives a whole new meaning to that bumper-sticker that reads, "Honk if you love Jesus." I have no doubt that part of the reason Jesus had the strength He needed to die on the cross was because of the visit and encouragement of Moses and Elijah. Lyndon Johnson's saying can easily be applied to Jesus on Mt. Tabor preparing to carry His own cross: "There are no problems we cannot solve together, and very few we can solve by ourselves."

Sometimes our support and encouragement comes from unexpected quarters. One day, two nuns were shopping in a grocery store and passed by the beer cooler. One nun said to the other, "Wouldn't it be nice to sip a cold beer or two on a hot summer evening?" The other nun answered, "Indeed it would, Sister, but I wouldn't feel comfortable buying beer because it may cause a scene at the checkout counter." The first nun replied, "I can handle that without any problem," as she picked up the six-pack and headed for the checkout. The cashier had a surprised look on his face when the two nuns arrived with a six-pack of beer. The nun said, "We use beer for washing our hair: a shampoo of sorts, if you will." Without blinking an eye, the cashier reached under the counter, pulled out a package of pretzel sticks and placed them in the bag with the beer. He looked at the nuns, smiled, and said, "The curlers are on the house." People encourage us in lots of ways, big and small, and sometimes they are people we don't necessarily expect to find in our corner.

We Christians are called to follow the example of Moses and Elijah on Mount Tabor, encouraging one another in our daily discipleship. Like those geese flying in the "V" formation, we should constantly encourage each other, cheer for each other, take turns fighting the wind-resistance so others can rest.

Here are some concrete examples: When you go to Mass, you're not just there to fulfill an obligation and then leave as quickly as you can to beat the Baptists to brunch! You should pray fervently for others. You have a role to play in your parish. Sometimes, you will have to encourage another parishioner who is going through a hard time, and sometimes, other parishioners will cheer for you when you feel you cannot go on. No one should feel like a stranger in their parish; everyone should feel welcomed, loved and needed.

Even priests need pep talks, and I once received a very beautiful one after running into one of my parishioners at the local athletic club. The next day she sent me this letter: "I hope this letter finds you well! It is such a pleasure to see you out at the gym taking care of yourself. My letter today is just to let you know that I am praying for you, and how I am praying for your continued health and well-being; that your prayer-life will continue to thrive; that you will be a good shepherd for your current and future parishes; that temptation may not get the best of you; that goodness and happiness may be yours." That was a pretty cool letter, don't you think? Now, can't you just hear Moses and Elijah saying the same thing to Jesus on top of Mt. Tabor: "Be a good shepherd, pray hard, don't cave into temptation"? It's just like Lyndon Johnson said: "There are no problems we cannot solve together, and very few that we can solve by ourselves."

By the way, this is why we Southerners say "all-a-ya'll!" You see, we belong to one another, and together we can go farther and accomplish more than we ever could alone.

¿QUIÉN MANDA AQUÍ?

Serving the poor as our masters and patrons

...

LUKE 16:19-31

Jesus said to the Pharisees:
"There was a rich man who dressed in purple garments
and fine linen and dined sumptuously each day.
And lying at his door was a poor man named Lazarus,
covered with sores, who would gladly have eaten his fill
of the scraps that fell from the rich man's table.
Dogs even used to come and lick his sores.
When the poor man died, he was carried away by angels
to the bosom of Abraham.
The rich man also died and was buried, and from the nether-
world, where he was in torment, he raised his eyes and saw
Abraham far off and Lazarus at his side.
And he cried out, 'Father Abraham, have pity on me.
Send Lazarus to dip the tip of his finger in water and cool my
tongue, for I am suffering torment in these flames.'
Abraham replied, 'My child, remember that you received what
was good during your lifetime while Lazarus likewise received
what was bad; but now he is comforted here,

whereas you are tormented.

Moreover, between us and you a great chasm is established

to prevent anyone from crossing who might wish to go from our

side to yours or from your side to ours.'

He said, 'Then I beg you, father, send him to my father's house,

for I have five brothers, so that he may warn them,

lest they too come to this place of torment.'

But Abraham replied, 'They have Moses and the prophets.

Let them listen to them.' He said, 'Oh no, father Abraham,

but if someone from the dead goes to them, they will repent.'

Then Abraham said, 'If they will not listen to Moses

and the prophets, neither will they be persuaded if someone

should rise from the dead.'"

Being a parish priest who has worked extensively with Hispanic Catholics, I've learned a lot from this community. They especially like to use one phrase that is loaded with meaning: "¡¿Quién manda aquí?!" Roughly translated, it means, "Who's in charge around here?!" The person who frequently asks this question is the father of the family, and the answer he expects is pretty obvious. He wants to hear his children say, "Of course, you're in charge, Dad!" And he wants to hear his wife say, "Honey, obviously, you're in charge." Now you know why "macho" and "machismo" are originally Spanish words. Regardless of its macho and chauvinist origins, it's still a good question to ask: Who's in charge around here? Who has the power? Who makes the decisions?

If I were to ask a Catholic parishioner who is in charge of his/her parish, what would they answer? Hopefully they've attended Mass regularly and could name their pastor and say, "Father is in charge around here." Others who have a little more understanding of the Church hierarchy might answer, "The bishop is in charge because he assigns the pastor and he can change pastors." Still others who know the Roman

Catholic Church even better might reply, "The pope is in charge." On the other hand, the more devout and spiritually minded among us might say, "Well, really Jesus is in charge, or the Blessed Mother is in charge." It's a great question, isn't it? ¿Quién manda aquí? Who's in charge around here?

Several years ago, I saw the hilarious movie *My Big Fat Greek Wedding*. In a very touching but poignant scene, the mother of the bride consoles her daughter. The bride gets cold feet and wants to back out of the upcoming wedding. Her mother shares a bit of motherly advice. She says, "Honey, there are only two things you have to know about marriage. First, the man is the head of the house. And second, the woman is the neck. And the neck can turn the head." You see, it always comes back to the same question: ¿Quién manda aquí? Who's in charge around here?

In the gospel above, Jesus tells the familiar parable of the rich man and the poor beggar, Lazarus. You've probably heard this parable countless times, but consider it from a different perspective. Ask the question: "Who's in charge in the parable?" Jesus creates two scenarios: the first one on earth and the second in the afterlife. If we consider the first scene, on earth, who's obviously in charge, who calls the shots, who has the power? Clearly, it's the rich guy. But in the afterlife, in the second scenario, who has the power and makes the decisions? Clearly, it's not the rich guy. I would suggest to you that in the next world, it will be the poor who are in charge. But notice it takes the rich guy a while to catch on, even in the afterlife. He starts ordering Abraham and Lazarus around, just as he was used to doing on earth. He commands them: "Tell Lazarus to dip his finger in water so I can cool my tongue. Tell Lazarus to go to my brothers and help them." Each time, however, Abraham says, "No." But notice that Abraham is not just answering the rich man's direct questions; he's also answering a deeper question that the rich man fails to ask: ¡¿Quién manda aquí?! Who's in charge around here?! Abraham is really explaining to the rich man, you're not in charge any more; you don't call the shots. As a matter of fact, Lazarus has the power and the authority now. As Jesus' parables invariably do, this story turns our earthly standard on its head. Priorities and persons and power structures in heaven are often the exact opposite of how they are on earth.

During the Feast of St. Vincent de Paul, we celebrate how he championed the cause of the poor. In one of his letters, he made a startling claim. He wrote, "With renewed devotion, then, we must serve the poor, especially outcasts and beggars." Hearing that, we may well react by saying, "Yeah, yeah, we already know that." But St. Vincent doesn't stop there; he raises the ante and says, "They" — meaning beggars and outcasts — "have been given to us as our masters and patrons." Did you catch that last part? The poor are "our masters and patrons." In other words, if you want to know who's in charge, St. Vincent de Paul would say, "The poor are in charge!" "¡Los pobres mandan aquí!" St. Vincent saw what the rich man in the parable was only slowly beginning to see: When you peer through the eyes of faith, through the eyes of eternity, things look a lot different than they do from a merely earthly perspective. Indeed, things are often the opposite.

Every time we pray the Lord's Prayer, the Our Father, we say a line that many of us rarely really grasp. We pray, "Thy will be done on earth as it is in heaven." Do you know what you are praying for? Obviously, you're praying for God's will to be done. But what does that mean exactly? What does God's will look like, practically speaking? It's not merely a vague desire for God's will to unfold in some distant and unknown future. Rather, we pray that God's will be done on earth AS IT IS IN HEAVEN. We might ask ourselves, how are things done in heaven, anyway? Jesus' parable gives us a glimpse: In heaven the poor are in charge. That's what St. Vincent was saying: "Learn to see the poor as your masters and patrons, and then you'll see a snapshot of what heaven is like." When we see the poor as our masters and patrons and serve them as such, we accomplish God's will on earth as it is in heaven. In heaven the poor will have loving authority over others, like Lazarus did. Who's in charge around here?! What a great question.

This coming week, look for a way to serve the poor. But don't serve them with a highbrow attitude as if you were giving a handout to someone weak and dirty, powerless and penniless. Instead, look at the poor you serve as your masters and patrons. Look at the poor like the rich man looked at Lazarus — in heaven. Here are some ideas. Volunteer to help at a food pantry or a place that serves meals to the poor. But serve them with profound respect and honor, remembering that in eternity, they will be your masters. Another group of people we might not think of as poor are the elderly. Just imagine how "poor" someone would feel if they couldn't drive, or remember things clearly, or bathe themselves, or put on their own clothes? This week, take time to call your grandparents and visit your elderly friends. But again, speak to them and treat them as if you were visiting Queen Elizabeth. The poor, the powerless, the beggars, the penniless, the elderly — they have all "been given to us as our masters and patrons."

Yes, the man is the head of the house. The woman is the neck. But the poor are our masters. Who's in charge around here???

THE "FAILURE" OF JOHN PAUL II

Working for communion and overcoming divisions

•••

EPHESIANS 3:2-3A, 5-6

Brothers and sisters: You have heard of the stewardship of God's

grace that was given to me for your benefit, namely,

that the mystery was made known to me by revelation.

It was not made known to people in other generations as it has

now been revealed to his holy apostles and prophets by the

Spirit: that the Gentiles are coheirs, members of

the same body, and copartners in the promise in

Christ Jesus through the gospel.

God always desires to bring together and unite, but the devil always drives apart and divides. Machiavelli once famously remarked, "Divide and conquer," and that's the favorite tactic of the devil, too. In fact, the Greek word "diabalein," from which we get the English word "diabolical," means "to divide." It is in the very nature of the Evil One to divide, while it is the nature of God — a Trinitarian "communion of persons" — to bring people into "communion," which means to be "in union with." You see, that's what God does because that's who God is, just like division is what the devil causes because that's who he is.

A friend of mine shared with me something that Pope John Paul II once said in private. Now this may be the stuff of legend, what's called "hagiography," but it's certainly consistent with the pope's well known words and actions. You know that John Paul II worked tirelessly to bring the divided and disparate denominations of Christianity back together, especially the Orthodox and the Catholics. John Paul II once surprisingly said, "If during my pontificate we do not achieve the reunion of the Catholic Church with the Orthodox Churches, I will consider my pontificate a failure." Wow! It's hard to imagine the papacy of Pope John Paul II a failure by any standards, but apparently the pope's own standard of success was the unity of the whole Church. Pope John Paul II understood well that God unites, but the devil divides, and he knew which side he wanted to be on.

In the passage above, we see someone else who comprehends the communion of persons that God desires, namely, St. Paul. See if you can catch the subtle argument St. Paul unfolds writing to the Ephesians: "The mystery was made known to me by revelation ... that the Gentiles are coheirs, members of the same body and copartners in the promise in Christ Jesus through the gospel." In other words, Jesus did not come just for the Jews, but to save everyone, including the despised Gentiles, who by definition were excluded from God's plan of salvation. The word "Gentile" refers to everyone who is not a Jew, the hoi poloi, the rabble, the masses, the Tom, Dick and Harrys of the world, the non-Chosen people. But the mystery that St. Paul sees is the same mission that John Paul II lived: to overcome divisions and bring people into communion with one another and with Christ. God unites, but the devil divides.

I once had a very personal encounter of communion with people of very different beliefs than me. I went to visit a terminally ill lady who lived way out in the Arkansas countryside. Only the lady who was terminally ill was Catholic, while the rest of the family was not only not Catholic, but decidedly anti-Catholic. I was pretty nervous driving down those country roads. All I could think of were old Jeff Foxworthy "You might be a redneck" jokes. For example, "You might be a redneck if your front porch collapses and kills more than three dogs." Or, "You might be a redneck if you mow your yard and find your car." Or, "You might be a redneck if you've ever hit a deer with your car … deliberately." As I walked in, I greeted the elderly mother and flashed my most comfortable smile at the rest of the family. As we conversed, the sick lady's brother interrogated me about my background. I said, "Well, I was born in India." He replied, "Well, we won't hold that against you." I smiled and said, "I don't hold it against me, either." But then he quickly back-peddled, saying, "As long as you don't hold us being hillbillies against us." I said, "Don't worry, your secret is safe with me" (and all the people I'll tell at Sunday Mass). But by the end of the visit, we had laughed together and cried together and, most important, we prayed together. I was so touched when the mother and the brother even hugged me before I left. That meeting wasn't exactly the fulfillment of John Paul II's vision of all Christians united, but it was a small step in the same direction. That afternoon, I learned in a very personal way how God unites but the devil divides.

Take a moment to really ask yourself whose side you are on. Do your words and your actions tend to bring people together or drive people apart? Have you ever noticed how seeing some people makes you want to go up to them and open up to them and get to know them, while other people make you want to run the other way? The first kind are people of communion; the second kind create division. Let me give you three tips to being a person of communion. First, smile more. When I was a new pastor, I received a pamphlet of "do's and don'ts" of a new pastor. On the top of the list was, "Smile more." A smile says, "I'm happy to see you. I am at peace. I want to share my joy with you. Everything is going to be OK." Besides, it takes a lot fewer muscles on your face to smile than it does to frown. Second, be humble. This might sound like an exaggeration, but I am convinced that nothing has caused more division in the world than pride. Why are there divorces? Why is there sibling rivalry? Why are there wars? Why is there ethnic cleansing? Why are there so many denominations in Christianity? Why can't our government get anything productive done? All of that is the pathetic production of pride. Because of our pride, we find it so hard to say things like "I'm sorry," or "I was wrong, you were right," or "Please help me, I can't do this alone," or "You don't owe me anything," or "I am so grateful for you." And third, pray together, like a Catholic priest once prayed with anti-Catholic hillbillies. My father never tires of saying, "The family that prays together, stays together." And that's absolutely true, because prayer makes God's grace the glue that holds you together with others so that nothing the devil does can divide you. And if your family is sadly already divided, pray for those members you feel far from. At least you can be united in prayer. A smile, a little humility and lots of prayer are the tools you need to be a person of communion, helping make the world a "communion of persons."

In 1995, Pope John Paul II wrote an encyclical that most people have never heard of, but it's my favorite. It was called *Ut unum sint*, which means "that they may be one," taken from Jesus' prayer for the unity of His disciples in the Garden of Gethsemane. Toward the end of the encyclical, the pope quotes St. Cyprian, saying, "I am reminded of the words of St. Cyprian's commentary on the Lord's Prayer, the prayer of every Christian: 'God does not accept the sacrifice of a sower of disunion, but commands that he depart from the altar so that he may first be reconciled with his brother. For God can be appeased only by prayers that make peace.'" Then the pope concludes, still quoting Cyprian, "'To God, the better offering is peace, brotherly concord and a people made one in the unity of the Father, Son and Holy Spirit.'" Keep that in mind, especially the next time you approach the altar at Mass to receive "Holy Communion."

THE KING AND I

Seeing the Church as Christ's Queen

• • •

JOHN 18: 33B-37

Pilate said to Jesus, "Are you the King of the Jews?"
Jesus answered, "Do you say this on your own or have others
told you about me?" Pilate answered, "I am not a Jew, am I?
Your own nation and the chief priests handed you over to me.
What have you done?" Jesus answered, "My kingdom does not
belong to this world. If my kingdom did belong to this world, my
attendants would be fighting to keep me from being handed over
to the Jews. But as it is, my kingdom is not here."
So Pilate said to him, "Then you are a king?"
Jesus answered, "You say I am a king. For this I was born and for
this I came into the world, to testify to the truth. Everyone who
belongs to the truth listens to my voice."

Everyone loves a wedding — even deacons. Not long ago, a deacon was doing a wedding rehearsal and the groom made him a very strange offer. He said, "Look, I'll give you $100 if you'll change the wedding vows. When you get to the part when I'm to promise 'to love, honor and obey,' and 'forsaking all others, be faithful to her forever,' I'd appreciate it if you just left that part out." He slipped the deacon the cash and walked away. The wedding day arrived. When it was time for the groom's vows, the deacon looked him right in the eye and said, "Will you promise to prostrate yourself before her, obey her every command and wish, serve her breakfast in bed every morning of your life, and swear before God and your lovely wife you will not even look at another woman?" The groom gulped, looked around and said in a tiny voice, "I do." Well, after the ceremony the groom pulled the deacon aside and hissed, "I thought we had a deal?" The deacon put the $100 back in the man's hand and whispered, "The bride's father made me a much better offer." So, deacons love weddings, some more than others!

Someone else who loves weddings and nuptial imagery are the saints. Why? Because they see "spiritual marriage" as the perfect symbol of the union of the soul with Jesus. St. Thomas Aquinas, as he lay on his death bed, did not want the monks to read the traditional prayers for the dying. Instead, he wanted them to read the Song of Songs, the Old Testament book of romantic love poetry, describing the love between God and the soul as a mystical marriage. That's how he looked at death. St. John of the Cross wrote profound poetry that was soaked with the sensuality of the spiritual marriage. You see, the saints love weddings, too, because they see the whole of earthly life as a kind of "spiritual engagement," and the end of life as the final consummation with Christ.

On the last Sunday of the liturgical year, we celebrate the Feast of Christ the King. It's placed deliberately at the end of the liturgical calendar as a reminder that at the end of time and history, Jesus will return as a King. But let me ask you: What is Jesus coming back for? To be sure, He's coming back to claim His kingdom; but He's also returning to claim His Queen. And the Queen is the Church. The esteemed theologian Dr. Scott Hahn described it like this: "[The Church] is the Bride of the Lamb, loved by him, redeemed by his blood and cleansed and sanctified by him that he might present her to himself." Then he makes this sweeping conclusion: "The heart of the universe, the goal of history, is love, romance, and marriage." Almost the last words of the Bible, Revelation 22:17, sound a similar chord: "The Spirit and the Bride say, 'Come, Lord Jesus.'" In other words, the whole Church longs for the return of Christ the King, for He comes to claim His Queen and the wedding bells will ring. English poet and cleric John Donne described death as the tolling of bells, saying, "Ask not for whom the bell tolls, it tolls for thee." Little did he know those tolling bells are also wedding bells.

Once while instructing my Latin class, I was explaining that nouns in Latin can be masculine or feminine or neuter. The book we were using explained that when you have a mixed group of people — boys and girls — that group is masculine. Of course, all the girls in class moaned, "more male chauvinism!" But I said not all mixed groups are masculine. When a group of people is relating to the world (to creation), that group is masculine, like the word "mankind." However, when a group of people relates to God (toward the Creator), that group is feminine. Just then, a particularly bright young boy raised his hand and said, "Like we are all the Bride of Christ!" I said, "You get an 'A' for the whole year!" His answer brought tears to my eyes. You see, Latin, like its daughter Romance languages, reveals that reality is at root relational — masculine and feminine; and not just relational, but also romantic (like men and women); and not just romantic, but also even nuptial; and not just the nuptials of any old couple, but ultimately, nuptials related to Christ the King and the Church, His Queen. That's why I love to teach Latin.

Now, you might be tempted to ask, "Who cares? What difference does any of this make?" Well, I think if you look at the Church as Jesus the King does, it makes a huge difference in how you live as a Christian. Do you see the Church as a "Business" or as a "Bride"? Is your idea of the Church a bunch of old men seated like CEOs in Rome making rules for the rest of us? Or, do you see the Church as the Bride of Christ preparing to meet her Husband, the King? When the Catholic Church went through all the scandals, a lot of Catholics left; Mass attendance dropped dramatically. And to be sure, there is no excuse for the pedophilia scandal. But if the Church is viewed as just an impersonal, monolithic institution, it's easy to walk away, as many people did. But other Catholics stayed and tried to make the Church better because they viewed it differently. There has been a surge in vocations to the priesthood; we have four men from our own parish in seminary. Three other men were just ordained as deacons, and at least two women are thinking about becoming nuns. Why did they stay? When you see the Church as a beautiful Bride, you want to protect and defend her honor. Because that's how Jesus sees the Church, as His Bride, and that's why He died for her.

A long time ago, I sent a poem by Elizabeth Barrett Browning to a girl that I loved. It didn't have quite the effect I hoped. But read this poem now, and picture Jesus saying these lines to the Church, His Beloved Queen.

How do I love thee? Let me count the ways.
I love thee to the depth and breadth and height
My soul can reach, when feeling out of sight
For the ends of being and ideal grace.
I love thee to the level of every day's
Most quiet need, by sun and candle light.
I love thee freely, as men strive for Right.
I love thee purely, as they turn from Praise.
I love thee with the passion put to use
In my old griefs, and with my childhood's faith.
I love thee with a love I seemed to lose

With my lost saints. I love thee with the breath,
Smiles, tears, of all my life; and, if God choose,
I shall but love thee better after death.

Indeed, Jesus will love us better after death because that's when Christ returns as King, and the Church will finally and fully be His Queen. Because you see, on that day, everyone will love a wedding, even more than deacons do.

WALK SLOWLY THROUGH THE CROWD

Giving time and attention to those around you

• • •

LUKE 10:25-37

There was a scholar of the law who stood up to test [Jesus] and

said, "Teacher, what must I do to inherit eternal life?"

Jesus said to him, "What is written in the law?

How do you read it?"

He said in reply, "You shall love the Lord, your God, with all your

heart, with all your being, with all your strength, and with all your

mind, and your neighbor as yourself." He replied to him,

"You have answered correctly; do this and you will live."

But because he wished to justify himself, he said to Jesus,

"And who is my neighbor?" Jesus replied, "A man fell victim to

robbers as he went down from Jerusalem to Jericho.

They stripped and beat him and went off leaving him half-dead.

A priest happened to be going down that road, but when

he saw him, he passed by on the opposite side.

Likewise a Levite came to the place, and when he saw him,

he passed by on the opposite side.

But a Samaritan traveler who came upon him was moved

with compassion at the sight.

He approached the victim, poured oil and wine over his wounds
and bandaged them. Then he lifted him up on his own animal,
took him to an inn, and cared for him. The next day he took out
two silver coins and gave them to the innkeeper with the
instruction, 'Take care of him. If you spend more than what I
have given you, I shall repay you on my way back.'
Which of these three, in your opinion, was neighbor to
the robbers' victim?" He answered, "The one who treated
him with mercy." Jesus said to him, "Go and do likewise."

Several years ago, I read a book by John Maxwell on leadership that had a simple phrase I'll never forget: "Walk slowly through the crowd." The idea was not to rush when you're with people; you should take time to stop and talk, showing genuine interest and investing time and emotional energy in other people's lives. Why? Well, because leaders lead people, not organizations. All leaders, and that includes pastors of churches, are in the people business.

One day, Maxwell had hired a new executive pastor at his church in California. On his first day on the job, the new guy walked right past John and all the people John was talking with and headed straight to his office. When John finished the conversation, he walked to the new guy's office and asked him, "What are you doing?" He replied, "I am getting to work!" John answered, "You just passed your work!" You see, the new pastor needed to "walk slowly through the crowd." I'm the world's worst at walking slowly. I'm usually in a hurry to get to a meeting or to my office, and I give people a quick wave as I fly by. After Mass while I'm greeting people, some people want to visit a little longer, but as I shake their hand, I actually pull them along and say, "Wow, that's great! See you next Sunday!" I have to tell myself daily and deliberately, "Fr. John, walk slowly through the crowd."

In the gospel above, a scholar of the law asks Jesus, "Teacher, what must I do to inherit eternal life?" Our Lord basically answers, "Walk slowly through the crowd." Jesus tells the parable of the man robbed and left for dead on the side of the road. Two people who should have taken care of him because they should know better — a priest and a Levite — pass by on the other side of the road. Can't you just picture them hurrying by the man pretending not to notice him? They did not walk slowly through the crowd. But a third man, a Samaritan, walks slowly, stops and takes care of the man. I imagine he talked with him, invested not only money but also emotional energy, and showed genuine interest in his welfare. You see, that's what Jesus means by being a neighbor, and that's what Jesus means by loving your neighbor. Walk slowly through the crowd.

Do you know another neighbor we often fail to recognize and invest time and energy in? That neighbor is Jesus. Every Sunday we say quickly to Jesus at Mass, "Wow, that's great! See you next Sunday!" How often do we rush through our lives, forgetting to slow down to spend quality time with Jesus? Believe it or not, even priests can ignore Jesus. A local pastor woke up one Sunday morning and, realizing it was exceptionally beautiful and sunny, decided he just had to play golf. So he told the associate pastor that he was feeling sick and persuaded him to say Mass for him that day. As soon as the associate left the room, the pastor headed out of town to a golf course about 40 miles away so he wouldn't accidentally meet anyone he knew from his parish. Setting up on the first tee, he was all alone. After all, it was Sunday and everyone else was at church. At about this time, St. Peter leaned over to the Lord while looking down from heaven and exclaimed, "You're not going to let him get away with this, are you?" Jesus sighed and said, "I guess not." Just then the minister hit the ball and it shot straight toward the pin, dropping just short of it, rolled up and fell into the hole. It was a 420-yard hole in one! St. Peter was astonished. He looked at Jesus and asked, "Why did you let him do that?" Jesus smiled and said, "Who is he going to tell?" So, don't forget that Jesus is also one of our neighbors and He doesn't like it when we ignore Him. Walk slowly through the crowd, because Jesus is in the crowd.

May I point out a few other neighbors we might be tempted to hurry by with the pretense of being too busy, like the priest and the Levite and John Maxwell's executive pastor? Have you ever reached out and befriended someone who is homosexual? You may have some strong opinions and feelings about homosexuality, but do you know anyone personally and have you heard their story? I'm not saying you have to change your feelings about the issue or that the Church must change her teaching, but can you be a neighbor like the Good Samaritan and invest time, interest and emotional energy in a homosexual person? Take another example: There may be very good reasons to have a double fence along the border between the United States and Mexico, and you may fight fiercely for that position and that policy. But have you ever been a neighbor and invested yourself personally in the life of an illegal immigrant? Perhaps you are strongly pro-choice and feel legal abortion is the last and largest hurdle to women's liberation. But have you befriended a woman who is passionately pro-life? In other words, can you be a neighbor to someone who holds the polar opposite viewpoint of your own personal and political convictions? What about someone on death row facing capital punishment? That's what it means to walk slowly through the crowd. I know those are some challenging words, but Jesus calls us to walk slowly through the crowd. Now, who exactly is in that crowd? Well, everyone is, without exception. That's your neighbor, and you must "love your neighbor as yourself."

WELCOME HOME

Forgiving others in order to enter the Father's House

•••

LUKE 15:1-3, 11-32

Tax collectors and sinners were all drawing near to listen to
Jesus, but the Pharisees and scribes began to complain, saying,
"This man welcomes sinners and eats with them."
So to them Jesus addressed this parable.
"A man had two sons, and the younger son said to his father,
'Father, give me the share of your estate that should
come to me.' So the father divided the property between them.
After a few days, the younger son collected all his belongings
and set off to a distant country where he squandered his
inheritance on a life of dissipation.
When he had freely spent everything, a severe famine struck
that country, and he found himself in dire need.
So he hired himself out to one of the local citizens
who sent him to his farm to tend the swine.
And he longed to eat his fill of the pods on which the swine fed,
but nobody gave him any. Coming to his senses he thought,
'How many of my father's hired workers have more than enough
food to eat, but here am I, dying from hunger.

I shall get up and go to my father and I shall say to him,

"Father, I have sinned against heaven and against you.

I no longer deserve to be called your son;

treat me as you would treat one of your hired workers."'

So he got up and went back to his father.

While he was still a long way off, his father caught sight of him,

and was filled with compassion.

He ran to his son, embraced him and kissed him.

His son said to him, 'Father, I have sinned against heaven and

against you; I no longer deserve to be called your son.'

But his father ordered his servants,

'Quickly, bring the finest robe and put it on him;

put a ring on his finger and sandals on his feet.

Take the fattened calf and slaughter it.

Then let us celebrate with a feast,

because this son of mine was dead, and has come to life again;

he was lost, and has been found.'

Then the celebration began.

Now the older son had been out in the field and,

on his way back, as he neared the house,

he heard the sound of music and dancing.

He called one of the servants and asked what this might mean.

The servant said to him, 'Your brother has returned

and your father has slaughtered the fattened calf

because he has him back safe and sound.'

He became angry, and when he refused to enter the house,

his father came out and pleaded with him.

He said to his father in reply, 'Look, all these years I served you

and not once did I disobey your orders; yet you never gave me

even a young goat to feast on with my friends.

But when your son returns who swallowed up your

property with prostitutes,

for him you slaughter the fattened calf.'

He said to him, 'My son, you are here with me always;

everything I have is yours. But now we must celebrate and

rejoice, because your brother was dead and has come

to life again; he was lost and has been found.'"

Let me ask you a tough question. Which is harder to do: confess your sins or to grant forgiveness to another? For small children, it's a lot harder to confess, to say, "I'm sorry I stole the cookie; please forgive me for lying to you; I'm sorry for punching Johnny in the nose." It's hard to confess and eat humble pie when we're young. But when we get older, other people offend us, and it's up to us to forgive them. I would submit to you that forgiveness is a lot harder than confession. I've counseled countless married couples, and the single biggest reason marriages fail is not because someone committed adultery, not because someone spends too much money, not because of a difference of religion. Rather, it's because one spouse refuses to forgive the other for some offense. Let me ask again. Which is harder: to confess cookie theft or to forgive an adulterous husband?

That's why people often miss the point of the so-called parable of the Prodigal Son. Who is the story really about: the younger son or the older son? Most people would say the protagonist is the younger son, but I disagree. The whole section about the younger son — the squandering money, the dissolute living with prostitutes — is setting up the real dilemma: Will the older son forgive or not? The parable really is not about confession, but rather about forgiveness. Why? Because Jesus knows which is harder for us (and which was harder for the Pharisees): It's a lot harder for us to forgive. After all, the younger son does finally confess his sins, while the older son stands stubbornly outside the house refusing to forgive — that's how the parable ends. We don't know if the older son ever went inside the Father's house. Confession is hard, but the younger son eventually does it; forgiveness is so hard that the older son can't do it. Alexander Pope wisely said 300 years ago, "To err is human, to forgive is divine."

As you enter confession, try to focus as much on forgiving as being forgiven. Ask yourself: Whom have I refused to forgive? Does anyone come to mind? I bet a lot of people come to mind: parents, siblings, friends, co-workers, maybe even a priest or two, oh, and how about your ex? I know lots of people come to your mind because plenty of people come to my mind, too, whom I refuse to forgive.

My friends, we reach a point in life when the purpose and perspective of the sacrament of confession change profoundly. We don't enter the confessional as the younger son — carrying the sins of sex, drugs and rock and roll — but rather we enter as the older son, weighed down with the burden of self-righteous indignation, grudges and resentment. To err is human — that was the role of the younger son; to forgive is divine — that was supposed to be the role of the older son. Forgiving is how the older son was supposed to become more like his Father, and that was the condition for him to enter the Father's house, but he couldn't. Forgiving others is also the same condition for us if we want to enter our heavenly Father's house. Can you?

iii.

GRACE

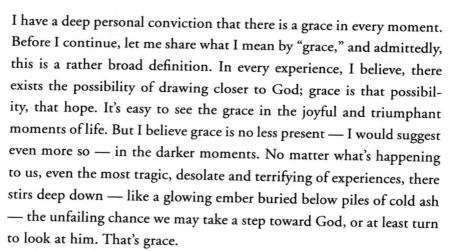

I have a deep personal conviction that there is a grace in every moment. Before I continue, let me share what I mean by "grace," and admittedly, this is a rather broad definition. In every experience, I believe, there exists the possibility of drawing closer to God; grace is that possibility, that hope. It's easy to see the grace in the joyful and triumphant moments of life. But I believe grace is no less present — I would suggest even more so — in the darker moments. No matter what's happening to us, even the most tragic, desolate and terrifying of experiences, there stirs deep down — like a glowing ember buried below piles of cold ash — the unfailing chance we may take a step toward God, or at least turn to look at him. That's grace.

Whenever I meet people passing through their own Garden of Gethsemane, I send them a prayer by 19th century Cardinal John Henry Newman. He wrote: "If I am in sickness, my sickness may serve God. If I am in perplexity, my perplexity may serve God. If I am in sorrow, my sorrow may serve God. He does nothing in vain. He knows what he is about." Newman was hinting at that hidden grace in every moment, the hope of finding God — even serving Him — regardless of how far we may feel from Him. St. Paul put it more bluntly, but with no less boldness: "Where sin abounds, there grace abounds all the more" (Romans 5:20).

The homilies in this chapter seek to find that subtle grace in those unsuspecting places and in those unexpected people. Several homilies touch on the topic of "prayer," which is the effort to heighten our sensibilities to God's grace everywhere. Other homilies cover how carrying the cross of suffering — when we usually feel farthest from God — can be an experience of profound, transforming grace. Others address the grace present in moving away from earthly occupations to be immersed directly in God, as well as how a simple word can provoke a torrent of grace. In short, there is a grace in every moment.

Gerard Manley Hopkins was especially aware of the grace hidden in every corner of creation, which inspired him to write his classic poem *God's Grandeur.*

The world is charged with the grandeur of God.
It will flame out, like shining from shook foil; ...

Generations have trod, have trod, have trod;
And all is seared with trade; bleared, smeared with toil; ...

And for all this, nature is never spent;
There lives the dearest freshness deep down things;

That "dearest freshness deep down things" is precisely what I mean by grace: that irrepressible hope that no matter how bad things get, no matter how far away we wander, no matter how dark the night, God always remains closer to us than we are to ourselves. There is a grace in every moment.

BRIDGING THE GAP

Asking the Holy Spirit to help us reach God

•••

JOHN 14:15-16, 23B-26

Jesus said to his disciples: "If you love me, you will keep my commandments. And I will ask the Father, and he will give you another Advocate to be with you always. Whoever loves me will keep my word, and my Father will love him, and we will come to him and make our dwelling with him. Those who do not love me do not keep my words; yet the word you hear is not mine but that of the Father who sent me. I have told you this while I am with you. The Advocate, the Holy Spirit whom the Father will send in my name, will teach you everything and remind you of all that I told you."

Let me share a little secret. Before I begin every homily, I always whisper this little prayer: "Come, Holy Spirit. Help me to say what Thou would have me say. Help them to hear what Thou would have them hear." After 17 years as a priest, I'm convinced that not only do I need the Holy Spirit's help to know what to say, but my congregation also needs the Spirit's help to listen and hear what He has to say. It's amazing

how what I say and what my parishioners hear can be two totally different things; my lips and their ears are like two ships passing in the night.
And we both need the Spirit's help.

One day after Mass, a young man said, "I really needed to hear your
sermon on mercy today." I replied, "I didn't say anything about mercy.
In fact, I didn't say anything at all; the deacon preached today, and I
don't want any credit for the deacon's sermon." Another Sunday when I
did preach a lady said, "That was a very good homily, Father." I sheep-
ishly said, "Aw, shucks, it was nothing. I give all the credit to the Holy
Spirit." She shot back, "I didn't say it was that good!" And then there
was the incident with Archbishop Fulton Sheen. At Mass, a lady had a
fussy baby that started crying during the sermon. Eventually, she stood
up and walked into the vestibule. After Mass, the Archbishop found
the lady and said, "Madam, there was no need for you to leave. The
baby was not bothering me." She said, "That's not why I left. You were
upsetting the baby." So, my apologies to all the babies I upset when I
gave this homily. What the preacher says and what the congregation
hears can be two very different things. But the Holy Spirit inpires us
and increases our understanding.

In the gospel above, Jesus tells the Apostles at the Last Supper the
Father will send them the Holy Spirit. Now, this may sound like an
unnecessary question, but why does the Father have to send the Holy
Spirit to the Apostles? I mean, they had spent three years listening to
Jesus every day, hearing His teaching right from His lips, seeing His
miracles live and in-person. Well, Jesus explains: "The Advocate, the
Holy Spirit ... will teach you everything and remind you of all that I
told you." In other words, Jesus is worried about the same gap I see at
every Mass: What He said and what the Apostles heard could be two
very different things. So, the Father sends the Spirit to bridge the gap
between them. How often they missed His point! They didn't immediately grasp what "rising from the dead" meant. No clue. How could they

understand how "there will be no marriage in heaven"? How many of us do? They struggled with teachings like "he who loses his life will save it, but he who saves his life will lose it." These teachings went straight over their heads when they first heard them. But at Pentecost, the Holy Spirit descended and the apostles finally understood and remembered what Jesus said. The Holy Spirit bridged the gap.

Here are the three things you can do to hear the Holy Spirit a little bit better. First, go to confession. Nothing drowns out the voice of the Holy Spirit like the voices of the evil spirits that lead us to sin. St. Ignatius of Loyola called this "the discernment of spirits," trying to figure out which spirit speaks to us. And if you haven't been to confession in a long time, the sins are piled up on your soul like so much manure; you can't tell what spirit is talking to you: the Holy Spirit, an evil spirit or your own spirit. Second, spend 15 minutes a day in silent prayer. I'm not talking about Mass or the rosary or even reading the Bible. Rather, just sit quietly in your room without the TV or radio, and listen. Blaise Pascal once said, "All of humanity's problems stem from man's inability to sit quietly in a room alone." I was once talking with our priest in residence, and he commented, "This is the first time I've lived in a house where the TV hasn't been turned on for a week." I'm still not sure if he meant that as a compliment. But in the silence, we can finally hear, we begin to listen deeply to the stirrings of the Spirit. And third, listen to the Magisterium, the pope and the bishops. Jesus said to the apostles, "Receive the Holy Spirit." We all receive the Holy Spirit, but Jesus said that in a way unique to the apostles. He bestowed upon them a special charism to be the conduit of spiritual truths, to be spokesmen for the Spirit.

In the seminary, I had some charismatic friends from Steubenville, Ohio. They often told me, "John, you just need to get a good dose of the Ghost!" I always said, "You know, that doesn't even rhyme: dose of the Ghost." But Jesus gave the pope and bishops a very special dose of the Ghost, and we hear the Holy Spirit through them in a way we can't hear the Spirit speak anywhere else. Coming to confession, seeking out silence and listening to the Magisterium help you hear the Holy Spirit, and He bridges the gap between us and Jesus.

One evening, I went to supper with a family from my congregation. Their 6-year-old son asked, "You can hear God talk to you?" I smiled and said, "Sort of. It's kind of how you hear voices in your head, but you have to listen very hard." Later that evening, I asked, "Is there anything I can do for you?" He immediately said, "Help me to hear God, too." And so, this homily is in answer to that request. But of course, what the rest of you heard in this message, God only knows!

CRAZY IVAN OF PRAYER

Listening to the Lord in prayer

•••

1 SAMUEL 3:3B-10, 19

Samuel was sleeping in the temple of the LORD

where the ark of God was.

The LORD called to Samuel, who answered, "Here I am."

Samuel ran to Eli and said, "Here I am. You called me."

"I did not call you," Eli said. "Go back to sleep."

So he went back to sleep.

Again the LORD called Samuel, who rose and went to Eli.

"Here I am," he said. "You called me."

But Eli answered, "I did not call you, my son. Go back to sleep."

At that time Samuel was not familiar with the LORD,

because the LORD had not revealed anything to him as yet.

The LORD called Samuel again, for the third time.

Getting up and going to Eli, he said, "Here I am. You called me."

Then Eli understood that the LORD was calling the youth.

So he said to Samuel, "Go to sleep, and if you are called, reply,

Speak, LORD, for your servant is listening."

When Samuel went to sleep in his place, the LORD came

and revealed his presence, calling out as before,

"Samuel, Samuel!"

Samuel answered, "Speak, for your servant is listening."

Samuel grew up, and the LORD was with him, not permitting any

word of his to be without effect.

Do you know what a "Crazy Ivan" is? A Crazy Ivan is a maneuver used by Russian submarine captains, and I learned about it watching the movie *The Hunt for Red October*. The Russian submarine called the Red October is being cautiously and closely followed by another sub, the USS Dallas. In order not to be noticed, the Dallas had ducked in directly behind the Red October. That would be comparable to a vehicle in the blind spot of your car's side view mirror. A sonar specialist on board the USS Dallas, named Jonsey, explains the maneuver, saying, "Russian captains sometimes turn suddenly to see if anyone is behind them. We call it "Crazy Ivan." The only thing you can do is go dead, shut everything down and make like a hole in the water." The only way to navigate underwater is by sonar, a device that picks up sound waves vibrating through the water. Sonar, however, is completely deaf to anything directly behind the submarine, and so the only way to hear anything in your "deaf spot" is to turn the sub to one side or the other and listen again. A Crazy Ivan lets you hear things you normally miss; it helps you hear what is hidden.

In the passage above, Samuel learns to listen to the Lord by doing a sort of Crazy Ivan in prayer. You see, until this point, Samuel had been deaf to the Lord's voice. And so, even though God calls Samuel two times, he runs to Eli, thinking Eli is calling him. Samuel innocently and ignorantly thinks the divine voice is a human voice. Finally, Eli realizes God is speaking to Samuel, so Eli advises him: "Next time you hear that voice, you should pull a Crazy Ivan." Eli was teaching Samuel that his usual sonar device — his ears and eyes and all others senses — would not detect the voice of God because God is often hidden in the "deaf spot." I remember Archbishop Fulton Sheen saying that most of us approach prayer with exactly the wrong attitude. We say, "Listen, Lord, your servant is speaking." We talk too much in prayer instead of listening like Samuel learned to do. Samuel learns to pull a Crazy Ivan, turning away from the normal noises and nuisances of daily life, and quietly listen to the Lord, hidden in his deaf spot.

One day, an inebriated Catholic ice fisherman drilled a hole in the ice and peered into it when a loud voice rang out from above, "There are no fish in there." The man walked several yards and drilled another hole. Again, the voice boomed, "There are no fish in there!" Then the man stumbled 50 yards away and drilled another hole. For the third time, the voice yelled, "I told you, there are no fish there." Finally, the fisherman looked up into the sky and asked, "God, is that you?" The voice answered, "No, of course not! I'm the skating rink manager." So, sometimes we pull a Crazy Ivan when we don't really have to: It's not God speaking to us, it's just the skating rink manager.

I want to teach you how to do a Crazy Ivan in prayer, how to listen to the Lord and hear His hidden voice. How many people complain, "I pray but God doesn't answer me," or "Why doesn't God just tell me what to do?" Well, most of us are like little Samuel and don't know how to recognize and hear God's voice; usually He's hiding in our "deaf spot." Now, to do a Crazy Ivan, you need to use what I call the three S's: silence, solitude and stillness.

First, silence. Ask yourself: Are there even five minutes of silence in my day? For most of us, the radio or the TV is always creating white noise all around us; there's very little silence. The movie theater proclaims before the show starts, "Silence is golden," reminding the audience to be quiet so they can hear the movie. Only when we learn to quiet our surroundings and ourselves will we hear God's voice. C.S. Lewis said, "One of the things you will never find in hell is silence." Why? No one there is interested in hearing God's voice. Silence is the first step of the Crazy Ivan.

Second, solitude. A good friend of mine who has three very active young boys said that the only place to be alone at home was in the bathroom. But even there, the youngest one will bang on the door and yell, "What are you doing in there?" So solitude is not easy to find. When we spend time alone, we quickly discover we're not alone. St. Augustine said, "God is closer to us than we are to ourselves." This reminds me of that bumper sticker I saw once that asked, "Do you feel far from God? Well, who moved?" God always desires to be close to us, but we keep running away from Him. In solitude, we begin to perceive how close God is to us, and we hear the voice of the One who is closer to us than we are to ourselves.

And third, stillness. By the way, this is the hardest of the three for me: simply to sit still and not move. But it's not just your body that you must quiet; you also have to quiet your mind and your thoughts, which is a thousand times harder. In order for a surgeon to operate, the patient must lie still on the operating table; so too, we must still the body and the mind so the Divine Doctor can heal our deafness in order to hear Him. Silence, solitude and stillness help you pull a Crazy Ivan in prayer and hear the hidden voice that spoke to Samuel.

Want to know what you will hear when you pull a Crazy Ivan? Want to know what God says when you finally hear Him? St. Teresa of Avila said, "His words are works!" That is, when God speaks to us, He changes us; His words go to work in us. Listen to her experience of prayer: "Only a few words were necessary to give me peace, strength, courage and security. The peace and the light that I received were of such magnificence that in a twinkle of an eye I was transformed, refashioned." The purpose of prayers is to make us better people; the litmus test of effective prayer is holiness. If you're praying well, you're also becoming more patient and prudent, more cheerful and chaste. On the other hand, if you give little time, energy and attention to prayer, you will make no progress in goodness and grace. If you practice 15 minutes of mental prayer each day — this Crazy Ivan kind of prayer — like Samuel you will hear God's voice, and like Teresa you will be transformed into a person who is more cheerful, charitable and chaste.

EYES ON THE PRIZE

Focusing our eyes on Jesus

• • •

MATTHEW 14:22-33

After he had fed the people, Jesus made the disciples get

into a boat and precede him to the other side, while he

dismissed the crowds.

After doing so, he went up on the mountain by himself to pray.

When it was evening he was there alone.

Meanwhile the boat, already a few miles offshore,

was being tossed about by the waves,

for the wind was against it.

During the fourth watch of the night, he came

toward them walking on the sea.

When the disciples saw him walking on the sea

they were terrified.

"It is a ghost," they said, and they cried out in fear.

At once Jesus spoke to them,

"Take courage, it is I; do not be afraid."

Peter said to him in reply,

"Lord, if it is you, command me to come to you on the water."

He said, "Come."

Peter got out of the boat and began to walk

on the water toward Jesus.

But when he saw how strong the wind was he became

frightened; and, beginning to sink, he cried out, "Lord, save me!"

Immediately Jesus stretched out his hand and

caught Peter, and said to him,

"O you of little faith, why did you doubt?"

After they got into the boat, the wind died down.

Those who were in the boat did him homage, saying,

"Truly, you are the Son of God."

I love sports: all sports, every kind of sport. I have even learned to enjoy sports that I used to think didn't deserve to be called a sport, like golf. Golfers have great little sayings, like, "Drive for show, but putt for dough." Or, "Hit the small ball, not the big ball," meaning, hit the golf ball (the small ball) and not the earth (the big ball). But of all sports, I'm partial to those that use some kind of ball, whether it's golf or basketball, baseball, football, volleyball or even wiffleball. The most basic skill needed in all these ball-sports is captured in the phrase "Keep your eye on the ball." Some baseball players are so skilled at seeing the ball when they're at bat they can tell by the way the weave on the ball spins whether the pitch is a curve ball or a fastball. You compliment a batter by saying, "Good eye," which means he kept his eye on the ball. Now, keeping your eye on the ball is hard to do — it's actually counterintuitive — because you naturally want to look where you're hitting the ball instead of at the ball itself. The top tennis players hold their heads steady on the ball, even after they swing through it. The first lesson in all sports with balls is to keep your eye on the ball. You don't just learn that lesson: It must become second nature to you, it must become instinct.

In the gospel above, Jesus is teaching the apostles the same lesson, not about keeping their eyes on the ball, but rather keeping their eyes on Him. We're familiar with the story about Peter walking on the water and then sinking. But if we think walking on the water is the main point, we've missed the whole point. Jesus wasn't interested in teaching the apostles how to walk on water: That's a small stunt of second-rate disciples. No, the real lesson is learning to keep your eyes on Jesus. If you do so, anything is possible, and nothing will sink you. You see, Peter was a neophyte apostle, like a youngster in legion baseball, still learning the basic lesson of being a disciple: Keep your eyes on Jesus. But eventually, it would become second nature to him, and he would keep his eyes trained on Jesus even as Peter was being crucified upside down.

Recently, we celebrated the Feast of St. John Vianney, who trained himself daily to keep his eyes on Jesus. He described prayer in these simple but sublime sentences: "When I pray, I go into the church and sit down in front of Jesus in the Tabernacle. I look at Jesus and He looks at me." I believe that is the best definition of prayer. Why? Because that is the best definition of love. Prayer is keeping your eyes on the One you love; prayer is keeping your eyes on Jesus.

Now, kids have a lot of trouble keeping their eyes on Jesus, and they are easily distracted. Two boys were walking home from Sunday school after hearing a strong sermon on the devil. One boy asked, "What do you think about all this Satan stuff?" The other boy replied, "Well, you know how Santa Claus turned out. It's probably just your dad." Those boys better learn fast to keep their eyes on Jesus. They're in for a surprise! A little girl was attending a wedding for the first time and whispered to her mother, "Why is the bride dressed in white?" The mother answered, "Because white is the color of happiness and today is the happiest day of her life." The child thought for a moment then asked, "So why is the groom wearing black?" That little girl should have kept her eyes on Jesus instead of doing fashion consulting! So, we have to be trained to keep our eyes on Jesus — it's very easy to get distracted

— until seeing Jesus becomes second nature, an instinct. We need to get to the point where we never take our eyes off Him.

What are you looking at these days? Are you keeping your eyes on Jesus? One year, our youth group traveled to Madrid for World Youth Day, and they got to see the pope. And the pope, the successor of St. Peter, told them to keep their eyes on Jesus. You see, the "successor" of Peter taught them to "succeed" like Peter! Sometimes we feel like St. Peter in the gospel story: One minute we're walking on water and everything is great, and the next minute we're sinking. We're hit by the winds of marriage problems, job loss, illness, or the waves of depression and loneliness and difficult discernment of a vocation wash over us and the ship of our life starts to sink. In those moments, keep your eyes on Jesus and reach out to Him. He will lift you up and calm the wind and the waves. There's a lot of talk these days about the end of the world. A priest friend of mine is really into this and has started a garden in his backyard with chickens and pigs. I called him and bought two chickens, a rooster and a row of tomato plants for myself. He's my "hedge-fund" manager. But of course, I am not worried about the end of the world; I'm keeping my eyes on Jesus. When your eyes are on Jesus, what difference does it make when the world will end? This is the main reason you should send your children to a Catholic school: We teach them first and foremost to keep their eyes on Jesus. The motto at St. Joseph Catholic School, for example, says it all: "I will try my best every day to learn, to love others, and to act like Jesus." Sometimes people compliment me on my homilies and say they love coming to Mass. Of course, I am humbled to hear that, but I am also worried to hear that. I wonder: Are you keeping your eyes on Jesus or on me? Here's the litmus test: I ask them, if I were no longer here, would you still come to Mass here? Keep your eyes on the prize. All neophyte disciples know the real prize is Jesus.

Next time you watch football or baseball or badminton, pay attention to how the pro athletes keep their eyes on the ball. A Christian's eyes should be that well-trained and focused on Jesus all the time. He's the only one who can save you.

HAPPY, HAPPY, HAPPY

Moving away from the world and closer to God

•••

MATTHEW 3:1-6

John the Baptist appeared, preaching in the
desert of Judea and saying,
"Repent, for the kingdom of heaven is at hand!"
It was of him that the prophet Isaiah had spoken when he said:
A voice of one crying out in the desert,
Prepare the way of the Lord, make straight his paths.
John wore clothing made of camel's hair and had a leather belt
around his waist. His food was locusts and wild honey.
At that time Jerusalem, all Judea, and the whole region around
the Jordan were going out to him
and were being baptized by him in the Jordan River
as they acknowledged their sins.

Last year, I received the strangest Christmas present ever: a book called *Happy, Happy, Happy* by Phil Robertson. You might know him as the father of the family on *Duck Dynasty*. What's even stranger is that I actually READ the book! Here's how Robertson describes his own version of happiness: "I have a God-given right to pursue happiness, and happiness to me is killing things: skinning them, plucking them, and then having a good meal." He continues by quoting Scripture, saying, "As it says in Acts 10:13, 'And there came a voice to him, 'Rise, Peter; kill and eat.'" Rise, kill and eat — that's my modus operandi."

Robertson goes on to explain that being in nature is about more than just killing things; it's also about his connection to God. He writes later on: "I always found a way to get back to God's most beautiful creation. Since I was a little kid, I've had this profound connection with and love for deep, dark unmolested woods. I think part of it is that there's no clutter out there — there are no computers or cell phones (at least not in my blind) and constantly updated information isn't being thrown at you from all directions." If you've ever watched an episode of *Duck Dynasty*, you know how religion is a pillar of the Robertsons' family life. They even go around preaching the Word. Each show ends with the family bowing their heads and praying before supper. In other words, being in the woods is not just about getting away from things; it's also about getting closer to God. You see, every step you take away from the busyness of the world is one step you take closer to God.

Every year on the second Sunday of Advent, we meet John the Baptist in the desert of Judea. Long before Phil Robertson wandered into the deep woods of Louisiana to be with God, John the Baptist sought the Lord in the desert of Judea. They were both doing the same thing, and each man saw the busyness of life as the main obstacle to closeness with God. John the Baptist belonged to a religious sect called the Essenes, who lived very frugally off the land and were extremely faithful to the Jewish religion. The life of the Essenes of the first century is described in detail in the Dead Sea Scrolls as intensely prayerful, revolving around the Scriptures, family-oriented and keenly watchful for the coming of the Messiah. In many ways, the Essenes were the *Duck Dynasty* of their day! As people came to see John the Baptist out in the desert, they, too, began to connect again with God, as they repented of their sins and were baptized. They felt what the Duck Commander felt: Moving a little farther away from the world meant moving a little closer to God.

When Advent season approaches, do you start to feel closer to the coming of Christ, or closer to the coming of Santa Claus? December should be a time of spiritual preparation for the celebration of Jesus' birthday. But, sadly, it's been hijacked and totally transformed into a time of material preparation: buying gifts, attending parties, decorating the home, traveling here and there. Now, these things are not bad, but they can often eclipse the spiritual meaning of the season. How ironic that throughout the whole year, we are never more busy than in December, when we should be the least busy, when we should be taking time for quiet and reflection and prayer. A friend of mine recently lamented: "Black Friday (with its frantic and fanatic Christmas shopping) is exactly what's wrong with our country!" I think both the Duck Commander and John the Baptist would wholeheartedly agree.

As December draws nearer this year, take time to prepare spiritually for Christmas. Sure, we can't all go into the deep, dark woods or out into the desert, but here are three things we can do: First, attend an Advent reconciliation service. Like the people going to see John the Baptist, we too should repent of our sins to prepare for the coming of the Messiah. Second — and this is my favorite thing to do — pray the rosary. I can't always pray the whole rosary at one time, so I spread it out over the course of a day: one decade on the way to Walmart, two decades as I go to visit someone in the hospital, three decades during the deacon's long homily at Mass, and finishing with the Hail Holy Queen while waiting for my chai latte at Starbucks. And third, carve some quiet time into your day. For 30 minutes, turn off your cell phone (yes, there really is an off button), turn off the TV, the radio, Facebook, Twitter, Skype, Instagram, LinkdIn, Tumblr, Bollwevel (they haven't invented that yet). Take time to stop, look and listen to the beauty of creation around you. Don't miss the small miracles that happen every single day.

Let me leave you with the lines of Robert Frost's famous poem *Stopping by Woods on a Snowy Evening*:

Whose woods these are I think I know.
His home is in the village though;
He will not mind me stopping here
To watch his woods fill up with snow.

My little horse must think it queer
To stop without a farmhouse near
Between the woods and frozen lake
The darkest evening of the year

He gives his harness bells a shake
To ask if there is some mistake
The only other sound's the sweep
Of the easy wind and downy flake.

The woods are lovely, dark and deep,
But I have promises to keep.
And miles to go before I sleep,
And miles to go before I sleep.

Everyone is busy, and has miles to go before we sleep. But we can still stop in the midst of our hectic lives and take a minute to enjoy the snowfall, to watch the woods fill up with snow. You see, every step you take away from the "busy, busy, busy," is one step you take closer to the "Happy, Happy, Happy."

ICE CREAM FOR THE SOUL

Using words to change hearts and humanity

• • •

JONAH 3:1-5, 10

The word of the LORD came to Jonah, saying:

"Set out for the great city of Nineveh, and announce to it the

message that I will tell you."

So Jonah made ready and went to Nineveh, according

to the LORD'S bidding.

Now Nineveh was an enormously large city; it took three days

to go through it. Jonah began his journey through the city, and

had gone but a single day's walk announcing,

"Forty days more and Nineveh shall be destroyed,"

when the people of Nineveh believed God; they proclaimed a fast

and all of them, great and small, put on sackcloth.

When God saw by their actions how they turned from

their evil way, he repented of the evil that he had threatened

to do to them; he did not carry it out.

MARK 1:16-20

As Jesus passed by the Sea of Galilee, he saw Simon and his

brother Andrew casting their nets into the sea;

they were fishermen. Jesus said to them,

"Come after me, and I will make you fishers of men."

Then they abandoned their nets and followed him. He walked

along a little farther and saw James, the son of Zebedee,

and his brother John. They too were in a boat mending

their nets. Then he called them. So they left their father Zebedee

in the boat along with the hired men and followed him.

Words are powerful things, and I believe the spoken word is the most powerful of all. In fact, I'm convinced words can cause more devastation than nuclear warheads and be more precious and pure than California gold. My former barber had a sign on the wall opposite the barber chair that read, "You shall have whatever you wish. Don't be hung by your tongue." I thought about that sign a lot sitting in his chair — I used to spend a lot more time sitting in barber chairs — and he and I frequently discussed the meaning of those words. What could be more wondrous than the words, "I do" whispered to the one you love and choose to marry? Nothing can change the course of history and heaven more than saying the words "This is my body" and "This is my blood" over humble bread and wine.

But everyday words can carry immense meaning, too. One day the chairman of a large corporation was late for a meeting. Bolting into the room, he took the nearest available seat rather than moving to his accustomed spot. One of his young aides protested, "Please sir, you should sit at the head of the table." The executive calmly replied, "Son, wherever I sit is the head of the table." John Maxwell, a leadership expert, says words can either help or harm a volatile situation. He writes, "Each year, I explain to my key leaders that they carry two buckets around with them. One bucket is filled with gasoline and the other with water. Whenever there's a "little fire" of contention within the organization, the leaders will either throw the bucket of gasoline on the situation and really cause a problem, or they will throw the bucket of water on the little fire and extinguish the problem." Words are powerful: They change hearts, they change history, they change humanity.

The Scriptures above demonstrate how words can pack a new punch when humans speak God's words. The prophet Jonah is sent to Nineveh to deliver the divine decree of judgment. But no sooner has he started his journey than the people immediately believe his message and repent in sackcloth and ashes. Their change of heart after hearing his words was quick and complete. In the gospel, Jesus doesn't just speak divine words, He is the Word. Remember when He said so long ago in the beginning, "Let there be light," and there was? Yes, that was Jesus who said that. So today, Jesus invites men to be His disciples, and like the Ninevites, they hear His divine Voice and drop their nets — and drop their dad! — to follow the Lord. You see, Jesus' words don't just reach the ears, they penetrate deep into the heart. Hebrews 4:12 declares, "For the word of God is living and active, sharper than any two-edged sword, piercing to the division of soul and spirit ... discerning the thoughts and intentions of the heart." When human words become God's words, they pack a punch.

An elderly couple took their grandson to lunch at a restaurant, and the 6-year-old eagerly led the prayer. He said, "God is great. God is good. Thank you for the food, and I would even thank you more if Nana gets us ice cream for dessert. And liberty and justice for all. Amen." Along with laughter from other customers, one woman angrily remarked, "That's what wrong with this country. Kids today don't even know how to pray. Asking God for ice cream. Why, I never!" The little boy burst into tears, asking, "Did I do it wrong? Is God mad at me?" The grandfather answered, "No, son, your prayer was perfect." Just then an elderly man walked by, winked at the boy, and said, "I happened to know that God thought that was a great prayer." Then added in a whisper, "Too bad that lady never asks for ice cream. A little ice cream is good for the soul sometimes." At the end of the meal, the grandfather bought ice cream for the boy. But instead of diving in, he picked up his sundae, walked over and placed it in front of the woman. With a big smile he said, "Here, this is for you. Ice cream is good for the soul sometimes; and my soul is good already." So, prayer is powerful, but if that doesn't work, try ice cream.

The spoken word of prayer is the most powerful thing in heaven or on earth, but how often do we pray? I'm as guilty of neglecting prayer as anyone. When I was a newly ordained priest, I promised myself I would never give people the advice, "Well, just pray about it." That sounded so cliché and more like an easy cop-out than effective counsel. But after 15 years of being a priest and seeing all my great advice turn out not to be so great, I more often tell people to pray about their problems. St. Monica was at her wits end on how to bring her wayward son, Augustine, back to church. For 30 years, she cried and complained about his behavior. She finally sought the advice of the holy bishop of Milan, St. Ambrose, who said, "Don't speak so much to Augustine about God, but rather speak more to God about Augustine." In other words, "pray about it." Ambrose gave the age-old advice to "pray about it," and the reason it's age-old is because it works. And when we pray for someone at Mass, we unleash power and peace like this world has never seen, because we join many voices and pray as one. Scott Hahn wrote in his popular book *The Lamb's Supper* this stunning statement: "The saints and angels direct history by their prayers. More than Washington, D.C., more than the United Nations, more than Wall Street, more than any place you can name, power belongs to the saints of the Most High gathered around the throne of the Lamb." So while you're at church, pray: Speak to God about the Augustines you know in your life. God's word is sharper than any two-edged sword. Your words reach people's ears; God's words reach their hearts. In prayer, human words become

God's words and reach their highest purpose and perfection.

You know, my former barber wasn't very good at cutting hair; his hands would shake as he held the scissors. But he was a very wise man who taught me the power of words. The words of prayer, especially those in the Mass, don't just change the bread and wine into the body and blood of Jesus: They change you, and they change me; they change everything.

JESUS SAYS "DO NOT WEEP"

Experiencing the healing and wholeness of Jesus

•••

LUKE 7:11-17

Jesus journeyed to a city called Nain,

and his disciples and a large crowd accompanied him.

As he drew near to the gate of the city,

a man who had died was being carried out,

the only son of his mother, and she was a widow.

A large crowd from the city was with her.

When the Lord saw her, he was moved with pity for her

and said to her, "Do not weep."

He stepped forward and touched the coffin;

at this the bearers halted,

and he said, "Young man, I tell you, arise!"

The dead man sat up and began to speak,

and Jesus gave him to his mother.

Fear seized them all, and they glorified God, exclaiming,

"A great prophet has arisen in our midst,"

and "God has visited his people."

This report about him spread through the whole of Judea

and in all the surrounding region.

One day, St. Joseph's deacon was at the horse races and losing his shirt betting. By the way, that's the reason you may have seen him mowing his yard without his shirt on: He lost it at the tracks. That day, the deacon noticed a priest who stepped out on to the track and blessed the forehead of one of the horses lining up for the fourth race. Lo and behold, that horse — a very long shot — won the race. Before the next race, as the horses lined up, the deacon watched the same priest bless one of the horses for the fifth race. He walked over to a betting window and placed a small bet on the horse, just to see what would happen. Again, even though it was a long shot, it also won the race. (The deacon has a hard time trusting priests, so it took time for him to catch on.) By the sixth race, he couldn't wait to see what horse the priest would bless. When he did, the deacon bet big on that horse and again, it won. Before the last race, he was so excited he called his wife and said he was taking all their savings and betting on the next horse the priest blesses. He couldn't exactly understand what his wife said, but she was yelling all excited, and he took that to mean "yes." Isn't it beautiful to see spouses communicate without words? But this time, not only did the priest bless the forehead, but also its hooves and eyes and ears. So, the deacon knew this was a sure thing. To his horror, however, as the horses rounded the track, the horse he bet on came in dead last. The deacon raced to the priest and said, "Father, all day long you blessed horses and each one won. But this last one lost by a Kentucky mile!" The priest peacefully replied, "That's what's wrong with you deacons; you can't tell the difference between a simple blessing and the Last Rites." So, a priest's blessing is a powerful thing: Sometimes, it sends a horse first across the finish line; sometimes it sends him home to heaven.

In the gospel above, we see another priestly blessing that has astounding results, too. Jesus is walking into a town called Nain and encounters a funeral procession coming out of the town. Let me point out two fascinating aspects of this remarkable episode. First, notice the details Luke records: It was a widow, the deceased was her only son and a large crowd was leading the deceased out of a city. Can you think of another occasion when that happened in the Bible? That's right: Jesus' own death, when a widow (Mary) was walking with her condemned, only Son (Jesus) out of a city with a large crowd (Jerusalem). I think Jesus experienced a kind of "flash forward" to Good Friday, when that would happen to Him. And seeing the widow of Nain, Jesus thought of His own mother and the sorrow she would suffer at His death, and He was moved to heal the son out of compassion for His mother and all mothers.

The second remarkable aspect of this story is that Jesus says, "Do not weep," with an application that has universal effect, as only He can. What do I mean? Jesus is, of course, addressing those words to the widow, but He's not just passing on a pious platitude, like when we say to someone who's sad, "Don't worry. It'll be OK. Time heals all wounds." Jesus backs up His words with a miracle and raises the widow's son to life. But Jesus' words are addressed not only to that widow; in a sense, He says that to all widows who will weep because Jesus is the Resurrection and the life. Ultimately, He says it to anyone and everyone who will ever weep. Why? Because only Jesus can make everyone's weeping stop by removing the very source of all sadness — death and sin. You know, we human priests bless with a little of that power that comes from the divine priest. Jesus' priestly blessing restores life and wipes away the tears. Only Jesus can truly and totally say, "Do not weep."

One Christmas I received a book from Archbishop Peter Sartain. I was feeling pretty special to get a book from an archbishop, until I discovered he sent one to every priest he's ever met. Oh, well, it's still a good book. In one chapter, he speaks of the importance of a priest's blessing. He wrote: "In recent years I have tried to be more attentive and intentional than I was in the past when offering blessings to those who ask for them. I give many blessings, and given the setting in which they usually take place — receptions, noisy rooms, parking lots — it is not always easy to concentrate." Now comes the good part. The archbishop continues, "I have realized, however, that there is great power (the power of the cross and Resurrection) and infinite love (the love of God poured out in Jesus) in a priestly blessing." In other words, every priestly blessing confers Jesus' own power and love. This is what the deacon was starting to see at the racetrack but didn't know quite how to cash in on. A priest's blessing, because it's really Jesus' blessing, wipes away every tear and trouble. Only Jesus can say, "Do not weep."

When the world makes you weep, who wipes away your tears? We do not always first turn to Jesus, do we? If I am honest, I have to admit I haven't always turned to the Lord's love and power to heal my hurts. Let me give you some examples of other things we turn to instead of Jesus. We can be tempted to turn to alcohol and drugs, and try to drown our sorrows, which only numb the pain but don't take it away. We try to distract ourselves in overwork, or excessive exercise, ignoring the pain and wishing it would just go away. Many young people engage in "cutting" with a knife or razor, deliberately inflicting pain on their bodies, which psychologists tell us is an attempt to cope with deep emotional pain, usually depression. Some lose themselves in thrill-seeking activities like extreme sports, again hoping the problems and pain will evaporate. Other people even turn to superstition or Eastern mysticism, hoping gurus and their practices will ease their pain. But none of these things or persons can ultimately say, "Do not weep." Only Jesus can. So, when you're hurting, seek Jesus' priestly blessing, first and foremost in the sacraments like Mass and confession, baptizing your baby or marrying in the church, or by asking a priest for his blessing. And we'll happily give it to you no matter where we are: in a parking lot or reception hall or in a noisy room.

You know, a priest's blessing probably won't help your horse to win the Kentucky Derby. But it will give you peace and healing in a way that this world cannot give. And if I were a betting man, that's where I'd put my money.

SNOWBALL'S CHANCE IN PURGATORY

Causing God's grace to fall from heaven

• • •

ISAIAH 55:10-11

Thus says the LORD: Just as from the heavens

the rain and snow come down

And do not return there til they have watered the earth,

making it fertile and fruitful,

Giving seed to the one who sows and bread to the one who eats,

So shall my word be that goes forth from my mouth;

It shall not return to me void, but shall do my will,

achieving the end for which I sent it.

One of the toughest jobs in television is to be the weatherman or weatherwoman. Sometimes we love them and sometimes we hate them. School children hang their hopes on every word of the weatherman when he predicts snow, hoping for a school cancellation. Grocery store managers stock their shelves on the weatherman's word that a storm will cause power-outages. People plan vacations and getaways only after checking the extended forecast. I've become friends with our local weatherman, and he says he gets angry emails and even threats when the weather turns out different from his forecast. One child refused to go to school one morning stubbornly saying, "The weatherman said it would snow!" A weatherman's words can cause joy or sorrow, they can give hope or bring despair, they can produce excitement or calm.

The Scripture above tells us that each of us has the power to don the mantle of the weatherman; in a spiritual sense, our words can make it rain and snow. Listen to Isaiah, who says: "Just as from the heavens the rain and snow come down and do not return there til they have watered the earth … So shall my word be that goes forth from my mouth … achieving the end for which I sent it." God's grace, His mercy, is like rain and snow falling from heaven that produce goodness and growth, that give joy and healing, to all the earth. And in the gospel, Jesus tells his disciples how to unleash this torrent of grace: by their words of prayer, like the "Our Father." When we pray for someone, we wear the mantle of the weatherman, and our words of prayer can cause the healing rain to fall from heaven, which brings joy, peace, hope and mercy.

For a moment, think of someone who could use a little spiritual sunshine, or maybe a child who desperately wants another snow day. Did you know saying a simple prayer for them can cause their spiritual weather pattern to change? A friend of mine sent someone whose mother had died a note of encouragement and included John Donne's powerful poem *Death Be Not Proud*. Do you think that brought a warm southern breeze to scatter the dark and cold clouds hanging over that man's heart? You betcha. Every week our parish sends acknowledgements to grieving families that multiple Masses are being offered for their deceased loved ones. The graces from those Masses can change spiritual weather patterns — even in purgatory. Recently, one person who died set aside $10,000 in his will for Masses after he died: He was hoping for some snow days in purgatory! But don't limit the heavenly rain and snow only to fall on those whom you love, but also pray for your enemies. Every weatherman knows that when he forecasts a sunny day, that sun will shine for everyone. It will even warm the faces of those who send him angry emails.

WE HAPPY FEW

Catching the grace of the moment

...

Matthew 28:1-10

After the sabbath, as the first day of the week was dawning,
Mary Magdalene and the other Mary came to see the tomb.
And behold, there was a great earthquake; for an angel
of the Lord descended from heaven, approached, rolled back
the stone, and sat upon it. His appearance was like lightning and
his clothing was white as snow. The guards were shaken with
fear of him and became like dead men.
Then the angel said to the women in reply,
"Do not be afraid! I know that you are seeking Jesus
the crucified. He is not here, for he has been raised
just as he said. Come and see the place where he lay.
Then go quickly and tell his disciples,
'He has been raised from the dead, and he is going before you to
Galilee; there you will see him.' Behold, I have told you."
Then they went away quickly from the tomb, fearful yet
overjoyed, and ran to announce this to his disciples.
And behold, Jesus met them on their way and greeted them.
They approached, embraced his feet, and did him homage.

Then Jesus said to them, "Do not be afraid.

Go tell my brothers to go to Galilee, and there they will see me."

As I mentioned before, I believe there is a grace in every moment, something that helps you to take one step closer to Christ. But there's a catch: To grab the grace of the moment, we must realize it's only available in THIS moment, not in a moment five seconds ago in the past, and not in a moment five seconds in the future. Grace is only available right now. Have you noticed how some older people are trying to catch "the grace of yesterday." They want to live in the past. How many people wish they were still 29 years old? They wish they were skinnier, didn't have any wrinkles, or gray hair, or suffer from arthritis. Young people, on the other hand, fall into the trap of trying to catch "the grace of tomorrow." They say, wistfully, "I can't wait until I'm in high school." Then, "I can't wait until I'm in college!" Then, "I can't wait until I'm married!" Then, "I can't wait until I have children." Then, "I can't wait until I'm no longer married!" Then, "I can't wait until I'm retired." And, finally, "I wish I were 29 years old!" We're rarely content with right now, with all the good, the bad and the ugly of our present lives. Theologian Scott Hahn said insightfully: "You know you've reached a high degree of holiness if you can say, 'Thank you, Lord, for all the blessings as well as all crosses you've given me. I don't want a drop more or less.'" Only when we focus on today — on this very moment — can we catch the grace to take a step closer to Christ.

In the gospel above, we see where all this grace comes from: It is rooted in the Resurrection, and from there it reaches every moment of time. It's Easter Sunday, and two Marys literally run into Jesus. They embrace His feet and do Him homage. Then Jesus says very curiously, "Do not be afraid." Why? Well, He wasn't just spouting off some blithe statement to assuage their anxiety. Instead, He was affirming the reality of the Resurrection, namely, Jesus is no longer bound by space and time, so He can be present in every place and in every moment. And when we run into His presence in every moment, we, like the two Marys, feel no fear. We read in 1 John 4:18, "Perfect love casts out all fear." When you embrace Jesus and feel His love, you feel no fear, only peace. That's the grace present in every moment.

Twenty-eight people received the grace of God and became Catholic at my church this Easter. But beforehand, one of those RCIA candidates received a very strong admonition NOT to become Catholic. A friend posted this on her Facebook page: "Please call me before you become Catholic! You are making a huge mistake! There is no way a man can forgive sins. The Bible has proven that the pope is the antichrist! The Bible is the sole rule of faith, and no church can tell you what to do." That reminds me of what Archbishop Fulton Sheen once said: "There are not a hundred people today who hate the Catholic Church, but there are thousands who hate what they THINK is the Catholic Church." Our 28 candidates were not afraid of such caricatures of Catholicism. They clung to Christ in the sacraments like the two Marys hugged His feet, and they felt no fear. Jesus' Resurrection made Him present that very Easter Sunday, not where they were the day before, not where they are today. They grabbed the grace of the moment they became Catholic.

Are you happy RIGHT NOW in your church? I'm happy. I wouldn't want to change anything in this moment in my life: not the good, the bad or the ugly. I'm happy I'm 45 years old this year (and not 29). I'm glad to be pastor of Immaculate Conception (and not bishop or pope). I'm glad I'm in Fort Smith (and not in Cancun). I'm content not having a full head of hair (well, I'm still working on that). I'm satisfied I can't play basketball like I used to (I had a great jump-shot). I'm happy not being married. I'm fine not winning the lottery. Because, you see, Jesus' Resurrection makes Him present NOW, in this moment. He's not waiting for us in some imaginary world of our wants and wishes — in some yesterday long ago or in some tomorrow that may never come. Shakespeare's King Henry V roused his troops before a decisive battle by telling them: "We few, we happy few, we band of brothers; For he to-day that sheds his blood with me, Shall be my brother; be he ne'er so vile, This day shall gentle his condition" (*Henry V*, IV, 3). The King knew there is a grace even in a battle facing overwhelming odds, and he didn't want his men to wish they were elsewhere. He wanted them to catch the grace of the moment. That's why college football coach Bret Bielema never tires of telling the Arkansas Razorbacks, "1 and 0" — because he wants them to focus on the game at hand. He doesn't want them worrying about the past or thinking about some championship game tomorrow. Grace is only available today.

Wherever you are, no matter how good or bad or ugly the situation may be in your life right now, God's grace is offered to you. You can always take a step closer to Christ. And when you take that step, you will feel no fear. There is a grace offered to you right here, right now, in this moment. Don't miss it.

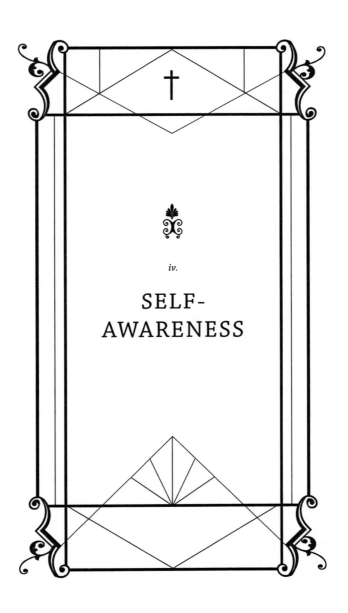

iv.

SELF-
AWARENESS

My university friends and I, stalwart liberal arts majors in theology, philosophy and literature, only took astronomy to fulfill the science requirement. One day, the professor took a tangent and emotionally described what heaven would be like for him. On the verge of tears, he said, "Heaven for me would be floating through endless space, constantly discovering new stars and galaxies forever and ever." My friend leaned over and whispered: "Now we know why he doesn't teach theology." Leaving aside the question of the true nature of heaven, my professor did hit on a deeply human desire: to explore, to understand, to know. Whatever else can be said about a human being, one thing is indisputable: We are insatiably curious.

Another arena of exploration equally vast — arguably even more so — is the depths of the human heart. Grasping this truth, Jeremiah, the Old Testament seer, wrote: "More torturous than anything is the human heart, beyond remedy; who can understand it? I, the Lord, explore the mind and test the heart, giving to all according to their ways, according to the fruit of their deeds" (Jeremiah 17:9-10). Both Dr. Olenick and Jeremiah understood a key insight: Whether it's the farthest reaches of outer space, or the darkest depths of "inner space"

— each person's human heart — everyone desires to explore, learn, rejoice and ultimately rest in the truth.

The homilies in this chapter offer assistance to those with a thirst to explore their own "torturous human heart," or in more modern terms, those who seek "self-awareness." Some of the homilies focus on discovering our hidden weaknesses, such as "Pride and Prejudice," "Born Blind" and "In a Blinding Splash." Others, however, help us see our gifts and talents, like "The Gift of Gab" and "Got Special Sauce." Each homily carries the conviction that we're a work in progress, slowly becoming the best version of ourselves, and suggests that self-awareness is an indispensable part of that process. We cannot become everything God created us to be without probing profoundly into that inner space of the heart.

Jeremiah assured us that we are not alone on this journey: "I, the Lord, explore the mind and test the heart." Jesus is with us. Surprisingly, as we enter within ourselves, we will find that Jesus has arrived long ahead of us. He has always been there waiting for us, in the depths of our heart, which turns out to be His preferred dwelling place. St. Teresa of Avila described this inner space as "a magnificent castle inside our own souls, at the center of which the Beloved (Jesus) himself dwells" (*The Interior Castle*). If you have the faith and fortitude to plumb to the depths of that vast, dark, inner space, you will hear that mystical, wordless conversation where "heart speaks to heart." That would be my description of heaven.

ALL THE WORLD'S A STAGE

Recognizing the roles we play throughout life

• • •

LUKE 19:28-40

Jesus proceeded on his journey up to Jerusalem.
As he drew near to Bethphage and Bethany at the place called
the Mount of Olives, he sent two of his disciples.
He said, "Go into the village opposite you,
and as you enter it you will find a colt tethered
on which no one has ever sat. Untie it and bring it here.
And if anyone should ask you, 'Why are you untying it?'
you will answer, 'The Master has need of it.'"
So those who had been sent went off
and found everything just as he had told them.
And as they were untying the colt, its owners said to them,
"Why are you untying this colt?"
They answered, "The Master has need of it."
So they brought it to Jesus, threw their cloaks over the colt,
and helped Jesus to mount. As he rode along, the people
were spreading their cloaks on the road; and now as he was
approaching the slope of the Mount of Olives,
the whole multitude of his disciples began to praise God aloud

with joy for all the mighty deeds they had seen.

They proclaimed: "Blessed is the king who comes

in the name of the Lord.

Peace in heaven and glory in the highest."

Some of the Pharisees in the crowd said to him,

"Teacher, rebuke your disciples."He said in reply,

"I tell you, if they keep silent, the stones will cry out!"

Shakespeare wrote the memorable line "All the world's a stage and all the men and women merely players." (*As You Like It*, II, 7) You've probably heard that, but most people are not so familiar with the lines that follow, and for my money, they probe even deeper into human nature. They read, "They have their exits and their entrances; and one man in his time plays many parts." One man in his time plays many parts. As I was growing up, my siblings and I certainly had our roles that we played in the family. My older brother, the firstborn, was the super-responsible one, making sure everyone was taken care of. I was the clown, the Shakespearean "fool," who entertained the rest of the family — not much has changed! And my sister was the youngest, the brooding princess that the rest of the family served. I bet each of you can look at your own families and identify the different roles each person plays.

Now, the interesting thing is we didn't always stay in the same role — we switched hats. Sometimes I was the super-responsible one, while my brother was the brooding princess (just kidding). One time, I was visiting with a local psychologist and a good friend, who revealed to me that as she talks to a patient, she always remembers that sitting before her is not only a 40-year-old man, but also tries to see that man as a 7-year-old boy (she imagines that boy sitting there), also as a teenager and, likewise, as a 60-year-old man. Her point was that each person is slowly growing and evolving, a work-in-progress. At any given moment, you're only seeing a snapshot of them in the long stream of their life. In other words, you are a little different today than you were yesterday, and you'll be still more different tomorrow. The ancient Greek philosopher Heraclitus said, "You can never step into the same river (twice); for new waters are always flowing on to you." You are constantly changing. Here's my point in all this: When we remember we're "merely actors" and that we change roles regularly, we can be a little more sympathetic with one another. How so? Well, it helps to remember that a given person is not merely the role they happen to play at that moment. Beneath the roles and the masks one wears, lives a human being struggling to live up to his or her exalted vocation to be a child of God. "One man in his time plays several parts."

Every Palm Sunday, we get the chance to participate in a play much greater than anything Shakespeare ever wrote. We divide up the gospel — the drama of the passion and death of our Lord — and each person gets a role to play and lines to read. I gotta tell you, I love being the priest because I only have to say the lines of Jesus. But over the years as a priest, I've also started to say the lines of the chorus, as well as the other parts. Why? Well, because I, too, have crucified Jesus with my sins, and yelled at times "Crucify Him!" I, too, have played the part of Peter and run away for safety instead of standing strong and suffering with my Savior. I, too, have betrayed Jesus with a kiss like Judas. I, too, have sought the politically expedient solution like Pilate instead of sticking to my convictions. I, too, (like the Bad Thief) have implored Jesus to come down from the cross, skip Good Friday and go straight to Easter Sunday. But occasionally, and these were in my best moments, I've prayed humbly like the Good Thief, "Jesus remember me when You come into Your kingdom." You see, one of the lessons of Palm Sunday, as we play these several roles, is to open our hearts to a profound empathy for one another. We should not just repeat the words of Peter and Pilate, but if we're humble and honest enough, we should recognize we've done similar things ourselves. Palm Sunday makes us sympathetic not only to Peter and Pilate, but also to the Pauls and Marys in our lives today. "All the world's a stage and all the men and women merely players ... and one man in his time plays many parts."

Someone who I believe lives this deep empathy for others is Pope Francis. He knows well that no matter what position or predicament or popularity someone has, it is only momentary, the role they happen to play on the world's stage at this time. Deep down they are a child of God struggling to be the best they can be. That's why Pope Francis made a phone call to the man who operates the newsstand where he bought his morning paper before he was pope — when he was known as Cardinal Bergoglio — and thanked him. Can't you just see his wife answering the phone and saying, yawning over her breakfast coffee, "Honey, it's for you. It's the pope." Breaking Vatican protocol, he invited the Argentinean President Christina Kirchner to lunch, even though they vehemently disagree over same sex marriage and distributing contraceptives. And on Holy Thursday, the pope celebrated Mass at a juvenile prison and washed the feet of 12 inmates. The pope is saying to each person he meets, and to the whole world, that, "You are more than the part you are playing at this moment on the world's stage, whether you're the president or a prisoner or a mere pauper. You are a child of God, and I love you." That is the point of Palm Sunday.

Take five seconds and think of someone you really dislike, or maybe even hate. Don't worry, it won't take you that long. Maybe it's President Barak Obama; it's amazing that some people positively despise him. One friend said she hates rich people. I told her, "I'm never giving you a ride in my Toyota Avalon again!" Others can't stand Bill O'Reilly or Rush Limbaugh. Some people don't like Catholic nuns, believe it or not. Two nuns were watching a baseball game, while three young men were heckling them from behind. They couldn't see over the nuns' habits. One said, "I would like to move to Utah. There aren't even 100 nuns there." The other said, "I want to go to Montana. There are only 50 nuns there." The third said, "I want to move to Idaho. There are only 25 nuns there." One of the nuns turned around, smiled and said very sweetly, "Why don't you all go to hell. There aren't any nuns there." So, don't hate Catholic nuns, and don't hate hecklers. You see, we are all a work-in-progress. We only see a snapshot of a person at any given moment. "You can't step into the same river twice."

In the book *Rediscovering Catholicism*, Matthew Kelly writes, "There is something ultimately attractive about men and women striving to become the best version of themselves." I love that phrase, "the best version of yourself." We play different roles as we're slowly evolving into the best versions of ourselves: the best version of Barak Obama, the best version of Bill O'Reilly, the best version of me, and the best version of you.

BORN BLIND

Inviting Jesus to heal our inner blindness

• • •

John 9:35-41

When Jesus heard that they had thrown him out,

he found him and said, "Do you believe in the Son of Man?"

He answered and said,

"Who is he, sir, that I may believe in him?"

Jesus said to him, "You have seen him,

the one speaking with you is he."

He said, "I do believe, Lord," and he worshiped him.

Then Jesus said, "I came into this world for judgment,

so that those who do not see might see,

and those who do see might become blind."

Some of the Pharisees who were with him heard this

and said to him, "Surely we are not also blind, are we?"

Jesus said to them, "If you were blind, you would have no sin;

but now you are saying, 'We see,' so your sin remains."

Many years ago in Nepal, two Buddhist monks were walking along a country path. They came upon a finely dressed woman at the edge of a river unable to cross. She was loud and obnoxious, complaining excessively about the raging river and the lack of a bridge right where she was standing. The older of the two monks approached the lady and offered to carry her across the river on his back. She agreed, but not very happily, grumbling along the way that her clothes would get wet. The older monk set her safely down on the other side, and the lady left in a huff, without a word of thanks. The two monks resumed their journey. After an hour of walking in silence, the younger monk finally burst out: "Why did you help that grumpy and garrulous old woman? She was so self-centered and annoying. She didn't even say thanks!" The older monk replied, "I put her down by the river an hour ago. Why are you still carrying her?" The younger monk had figuratively carried the woman much farther than the older monk. He could see the faults in the old woman, but he was blind to his own bitterness, resentment and anger. Someone asked Helen Keller once if there was anything worse than being born blind. She answered, "Having sight, but without vision." That's what the younger monk suffered: He could see, but he lacked a penetrating vision and perception into himself.

In the gospel above, Jesus wants to help people have both sight and vision, and especially the vision of faith. You see, faith is a kind of "double vision" that allows us not only to understand who God is, but also to see ourselves better. John Paul II frequently said Jesus came not only to reveal the mystery of who God is, but also the mystery of who man and woman are. Jesus cured the blind man and gave him faith, and that's why the blind man worshiped Jesus. With the eyes of faith he could see that Jesus was not only a man, but also God. Jesus wanted to give the Pharisees the gift of faith, too, because they suffered from an inner blindness. They knew plenty about God, but they woefully lacked self-awareness, especially about their sins. Like the older monk helped the younger monk to see his blindness, so Jesus tried to help the Pharisees, but they refused. Therefore, Jesus sadly declares, "I came into this world for judgment, so that those who do not see might see, and those who do see might become blind." The "double vision" of faith helps us see that Jesus is the light of the world, but also that everyone is born blind to their sins. Faith aids us in seeing not only who Jesus is, but also who we are.

Here's a little joke to lighten things up a bit. Several years ago, an Irish priest was driving from Connecticut to New York and was stopped by a state trooper for speeding. The state trooper smelled alcohol on the priest's breath and saw an empty wine bottle on the floor of the car. He asked, "Sir, have you been drinking?" The priest replied, "No, I haven't lad, I've just been sipping plain water." The trooper asked again, "Then why do I smell wine?" The priest looked at the bottle and exclaimed, "Glory be to God! He's done it again!" Now, for the record, that priest was not me. The state trooper could see the priest's sins, but the priest was blind to them.

Let me ask you a tough question: Do you have sight but lack vision, especially the vision of faith? Our faith helps us know God, and we do know a lot about Him. But faith also should help us to know ourselves. But do we? How easily we see other people's sins and vices, their faults and failures, yet remain ignorant about our own. Archbishop Fulton Sheen jokingly said, "It used to be that only Catholics believed in the Immaculate Conception. Now, EVERYONE believes that he is 'immaculately conceived!' Everyone thinks he's sinless. Our own sins and vices are like halitosis — everyone else can smell our bad breath, but we think our breath smells like roses. It never fails when a couple comes to see me for marriage counseling: Each person can see so clearly and obviously the faults of the other, but have hardly any awareness of their own weaknesses and flaws. Once I gently pointed out to someone, "You have some areas you could work on." He said, "No I don't." I suggested that he was denying his issues. He fired back, "No, I'm not." I said, "Dude, you just denied your denial." He insisted, "No I didn't." I said, "OK. I guess we're done here." Trying to see our own sins is like a dog trying to catch its own tail: We run in circles, and no matter how fast we run, we can't quite grab it.

I am convinced this is why more Catholics don't go to confession. It's because we can't see our own sins; and because we can't see our sins, we think we don't have any. If you seriously want to know your own sins and failings, here's a foolproof way to find them. Turn to your spouse and say, "Honey, I honestly cannot think of anything I do wrong that I need to confess. I really can't. If you could make a list of my sins — which I'm sure would be very short and very sweet because of course there really aren't any — I'll be happy to confess them." What do you think would happen? You'd have the happiest spouse in the world. Children should say that to their parents, and parents to their children. Priests should say that to their staff! How easily other people can see we are jealous and lazy, we are gossips and greedy, we are vain and self-righteous, we are arrogant and condescending. If people prepared lists of sins for each other, our Saturday confession lines would stretch all the way around the block! But like that young monk, we'd rather talk about the angry and acerbic old lady at the riverbank than look at our own flaws and failures.

Is there anything worse than being born blind? Yes, there is: to have sight but no vision, especially to lack the vision of faith. The "double vision" of faith not only helps us to see who God is, but also to see who we are. And that faith opens our eyes to one simple fact: We are all born blind.

GOT SPECIAL SAUCE?

Becoming the food that nourishes the world

•••

Matthew 14:13-21

When Jesus heard of the death of John the Baptist,

he withdrew in a boat to a deserted place by himself.

The crowds heard of this and followed him on foot

from their towns. When he disembarked and saw the vast crowd,

his heart was moved with pity for them, and he cured their sick.

When it was evening, the disciples approached him and said,

"This is a deserted place and it is already late;

dismiss the crowds so that they can go to the villages and buy

food for themselves."

Jesus said to them, "There is no need for them to go away;

give them some food yourselves." But they said to him,

"Five loaves and two fish are all we have here."

Then he said, "Bring them here to me, "

and he ordered the crowds to sit down on the grass.

Taking the five loaves and the two fish,

and looking up to heaven, he said the blessing,

broke the loaves, and gave them to the disciples,

who in turn gave them to the crowds.

They all ate and were satisfied, and they picked up the
fragments left over — twelve wicker baskets full.
Those who ate were about five thousand men, not counting
women and children.

We all have different relationships with food. Some people love food and even dream of their next meal, while others see it as just another necessity of life and scarf down their food as fast as possible. That's why we have fast-food restaurants. I lived in a Franciscan monastery while studying in Washington, D.C., where a Franciscan monk did the culinary duties. When someone complimented his cooking, he always replied, "Well, it will keep body and soul together." Not a very high standard. You're not going to see him anytime soon on *Throwdown with Bobby Flay*. Now, a friend and fellow priest of mine has a very different approach to food. He likes to eat at restaurants where there's an all-you-can-eat buffet. He says, "When we eat at a buffet restaurant, we Indians will take a lot of food. We must do justice when we eat." By that he means you should eat for a profit; eat more than you pay for. When I return home to visit my parents in Little Rock, Ark., I'll stay for lunch or supper. My father invariably takes a fork-full of food from his own plate and puts it on mine. At first, I used to say, "No, Dad, I've got enough on my plate." But now I understand his gesture as a loving symbol of his affection for his thick-headed son, and I gladly accept. We all relate to food differently: Eating can mean as little as putting gas in your car, or it can be as saturated with significance as the Last Supper.

In the gospel above, Jesus shows His disciples yet another way to relate to food, how He relates to food: He actually becomes the food. It's been a long day out on the preaching circuit and the apostles are beat. Exhausted, they inform Jesus, "Dismiss the crowds so that they can go to the villages and buy food for themselves." Do you remember Jesus' reply? He said, "Give them some food yourselves." And they bring five loaves and two fish. But they actually missed His real point because they took His words literally. You see, for Jesus, the real food people need is not so much material as it is spiritual, not so much for their stomachs as for their souls, and that food is the Good News of the Gospel which the apostles must be ready to preach even when they're tired. In other words, the real food was not bread and fish but the bodies and spirits, the faith, courage and joy of the apostles themselves. They must become the food; they must feed people with their tireless love.

When I first arrived at St. Raphael, which had 18,000 parishioners, the out-going pastor gave me a little advice. He said, "John, take care of yourself. If you're not careful, these people will eat you alive." He was warning me that the sheer size of the congregation could be over-whelming, not that they were cannibals. Now, what he said was true and important: A priest must take time for proper rest and recharging. But on the other hand, in a spiritual sense, a priest is also supposed to be the food that feeds the people: His body, his spirit, his love, his faith, his joy also nourish the people. Don't you know priests who fed you with all that they are? Archbishop Fulton Sheen said that the words of consecration — the part where the priest takes the bread and says, "This is my body" — have a two-fold meaning. The first and primary meaning is that he speaks in the person of Jesus. Jesus through the priest says, "This is my *body*," and so the bread becomes the Body of Christ, which nourishes us. But the secondary meaning is that the priest speaks on his own behalf, and so those words also mean, "This is *my* body," which will be given up for you. The priest announces to all that he must become spiritual food for the people. We all relate to food differently, but when you follow the example of Jesus, you don't just relate to food, you become the food.

Now, not all cooks are created equal, especially when the cooks are grandmas. I once heard a story about little Johnny and his family having Sunday supper at his grandparents' house. Everyone was seated around the table as the food was served. When little Johnny received his plate, he started eating right away. His mother scolded him, "Johnny, please wait until we say our prayer." Johnny answered, "I don't need to." His mother insisted, "We always pray before eating at our house." Johnny smiled as he said, "But that's at our house. This is Grandma's house, and she knows how to cook." Have you ever wondered why grandmas always cook so much better? It's because they have a secret ingredient in their recipe: It's their love. They put their heart into the meal, and in that way they have become part of the food.

Did you ever think Jesus was asking you to give the world something to eat? I'm not talking about serving the hungry of the world Cheerios and cheesecake. I am convinced that Jesus is calling each Christian, in a spiritual but very real sense, to become the food that feeds the world. Because, each of you has received a special gift — a unique grace — that the world is hungry for. Fortune 500 companies hire recruiters called headhunters. One headhunter approached a good friend of mine, who's a vice president, and asked, "What's your special sauce?" In other words, what makes you unique and successful? What special flavor do you add to this company? Young men think they could never be a priest because they have nothing to offer. Well, they don't know what their "special sauce" is and how much the Church would be nourished by it. How many Catholics sit on the sidelines of parish life, afraid to get involved as lectors or Eucharistic ministers, help with youth ministry, assist with prison ministry, or go on mission trips? You see, being a good Catholic requires more than just coming to Mass and giving money in the collection. We used to say that all Catholics have to do is "pray, pay and obey." But in the gospel today, Jesus insists that his disciples must do more. Why? Because each person, without exception, has received a unique grace, a special sauce, and only you can add that flavor to the Banquet of

Life Jesus has prepared for the world.

Jesus says in the gospel above: "You give them some food your-selves." Now, say those words slowly to yourself, but pause before you say the last word: "You give them some food ... yourselves."

IN A BLINDING SPLASH

Discovering our true selves

...

LUKE 5:1-11

While the crowd was pressing in on Jesus and listening to the
word of God, he was standing by the Lake of Gennesaret.
He saw two boats there alongside the lake;
the fishermen had disembarked and were washing their nets.
Getting into one of the boats, the one belonging to Simon,
he asked him to put out a short distance from the shore.
Then he sat down and taught the crowds from the boat.
After he had finished speaking, he said to Simon,
"Put out into deep water and lower your nets for a catch."
Simon said in reply,
"Master, we have worked hard all night and have caught nothing,
but at your command I will lower the nets."
When they had done this, they caught a great number of fish
and their nets were tearing. They signaled to their partners in
the other boat to come to help them. They came and filled both
boats so that the boats were in danger of sinking.
When Simon Peter saw this, he fell at the knees of
Jesus and said,

"Depart from me, Lord, for I am a sinful man."

For astonishment at the catch of fish they had made

seized him and all those with him, and likewise James and John,

the sons of Zebedee, who were partners of Simon.

Jesus said to Simon, "Do not be afraid; from now on you

will be catching men."

When they brought their boats to the shore,

they left everything and followed him.

Every now and then, in a blinding flash, we see ourselves as we really are, not as we think we are, or as we would like to be. Archbishop Fulton Sheen said every person can see his or her reflection in three pools of water. In the first pool, we see ourselves as we think we look. We think, "Hey, I look pretty good." In the second pool of water, we see our reflection as the world sees us. I always remember the advice a wise teacher gave the parents of his students. He cautioned, "If you don't believe everything your children say happens in class, I won't believe everything they say happens at home." Good advice. So, other people's opinions fill the second pool of water we look into. And in the third pool, we see ourselves as God sees us, that is, as we truly are. But most of the time, we walk through the world thinking we're like Dorian Gray. Remember him? *The Picture of Dorian Gray* was the only novel written by Oscar Wilde, in which a strikingly handsome young man — not unlike myself — actually sells his soul in order to stay good looking. But down in the basement, a painted picture of him suffers all the ravages of his sins and old age. How many of us see ourselves as we truly are?

One night an elderly man paid a surprise visit to his son and his family. Tired from a long day's walk, he was relieved to finally ring the doorbell. The young man who opened the door was clearly unhappy by the unannounced visit and with a strained smile said, "Hi, Dad,

165

what are you doing here?" The old man sighed, "Well, I wanted to stop by and see the family." The young man hesitated, "Well, the family is in bed and we've cleared the supper table. I don't think tonight is a good time for a visit." The old man smiled, "I didn't mean to bother you. Mind if I just rest a bit on the front porch before I head back?" The young man, still perturbed, said, "Well, OK." Then he ordered his 7-year-old son to bring a sheet from the closet for the old man to wrap himself up in. When the little boy came back, he had cut the sheet in two pieces. The father gasped, "Son, why did you do that?" The little boy replied, "One piece is for grandpa. And I'll save the other piece for when you come to visit me someday." In a blinding flash, we see who we really are. Our picture, like that of Dorian Gray, isn't very pretty.

In the Gospel pericope above, Jesus pays a surprise visit to St. Peter, and what Peter sees isn't pretty either. Jesus tells Peter to put his boat into deep water and throw in the nets for a catch. There's a miraculous catch of fish. But more is going on below the surface of the story, just like there's more going on below the surface of the lake, than Peter can see. Jesus is really telling Peter to put out into the deep, not only into the lake, but also into his own heart. And when Peter peers over the side of the boat into the pool of Gennesaret, he sees his true reflection, his sinfulness. He sees himself as God sees him. So Peter immediately exclaims, "Depart from me, Lord, for I am a sinful man." Peter saw his own "Picture of Dorian Gray," you might say, the real face he was hiding from the world. But Jesus assures him, "Be not afraid, I can help you be yourself again." Jesus healed Peter's sinfulness and helped him to see who he really was.

A little girl was sitting in her grandfather's lap as he read her a bedtime story. From time to time, she would take her eyes off the book and reach up to touch his wrinkled cheek. She was alternately stroking her own cheek, then his again. Finally, she spoke up, "Grandpa, did God make you?" "Yes, sweetheart," he answered, "God made me a long time ago." "Oh," she paused, "Grandpa, did God make me, too?" "Yes, indeed, honey," he said, "God made you just a little while ago." Feeling their respective faces again, the little girl observed, "God's getting better at it, isn't He?" Yes, God's getting better at it; He is slowly and gently improving our faces, erasing the sins and sadness of Dorian Gray and repainting our true picture as a child of God.

Do you know who you really are? Most of us would probably say, "Of course I do! I'm the knight in shining armor! I'm the beautiful princess bride!" And, you know, sometimes we go to incredible lengths and enormous expense to look perfect and play that part. But is that who we really are? I'll never forget what that great theologian Johnny Depp once said: "Gravity is going to get us all!" So, may I suggest that instead of getting stuck staring into that first pool of our own perceptions, let the Lord lead you into the deep waters, the pool that reflects what God sees, even if you see your sins and sadness.

I tell couples I prepare for marriage to get to know each other well — their warts, their weaknesses and their wild hairs! I say, "The worst thing that can happen to you on your wedding day is that you marry a stranger, someone you don't really know. On the other hand, be really honest with each other. Just imagine how you'd feel on your wedding day if you could say to each other, 'Honey, I know you're not the knight in shining armor. But I want to marry you anyway.' How wonderful would it feel for someone to truly know you and still want to spend their life with you?" By the way, that would never happen to Dorian Gray, because no one truly and deeply knew him.

Carl Jung once observed, "Deep down, below the surface of the average man's conscience, he hears a voice whispering, 'There is something not right,' no matter how much his rightness is supported by public opinion or moral code." In other words, the first two pools do not reveal our deepest identity. Only Jesus can lead us to that third pool, where we see ourselves as we really are; in God's eyes, we see our sins and our stupidity. A Carmelite priest once told me that in quiet prayer, we get to know Jesus, but we also discover ourselves, and that's why it's so hard to pray: we don't much like what we see. Jesus always leads us to that third pool, where we see who we really are.

Every year we are blessed with the liturgical season of Lent. Every Lent, ask Jesus to help you "put out into the deep water," to peer into that pool of how God sees you. Sometimes in a blinding flash — actually in a blinding splash! — we see ourselves as we really are.

MINE, OURS, YOURS

Letting go of ourselves and holding on to Christ

•••

1 PETER 1:14-16

Therefore, gird up the loins of your mind, live soberly,

and set your hopes completely on the grace to be brought to you

at the revelation of Jesus Christ. Like obedient children,

do not act in compliance with the desires of your former igno-

rance but, as He who called you is holy,

be holy yourselves in every aspect of your conduct,

for it is written, Be holy because I am holy.

MARK 10:28-31

Peter began to say to Jesus,

"We have given up everything and followed you."

Our former bishop, now Archbishop of Seattle, J. Peter Sartain, once described how we go through three stages of Christian maturity. In each stage, we tend to use a peculiar word. In the first stage we say "mine." This lowest level is usually that of a child. The bishop said: "'Mine' is typically a word spoken with quivering lips and the tenacious tug of little hands. 'Mine' is a fighting word, rarely spoken in hushed tones." I say that word every morning as I grab the coffee pot from our associate priest: "Mine!" The second stage often uses the word "ours." He explained: "'Ours' is a civil word, a family word, one that can hold us in pretty good stead through most of life." But the last stage is when we humbly say "yours." The bishop continued, "There comes a time, especially in our relationship with God, when, with empty hands open in poverty, we say only this: 'Everything is yours. I can't do it. Will you do it for me and in me ... as you always have?'" These three words correspond beautifully to the three stages of the spiritual life the classic authors taught. "Mine" refers to the purgative way, where we learn to confront and conquer our sinful selves. "Ours" is like the illuminative way because it indicates that we're growing in awareness of others and the need to love others. And "yours" is the counterpart of the unitive way because it is complete abandonment to God. "All is yours," we finally say. Or, as John the Baptist put it perfectly: "I must decrease and He must increase." Mine. Ours. Yours.

We see Peter going through these stages in the readings above. In the gospel, Peter pines, "We have given up everything to follow you." It's as if he's complaining: "I've given up everything that is mine, and now I have nothing." Can't you almost picture Peter saying that with quivering lips? But in his first letter as our first pope, written much later, we see Peter in the full blossom of Christian maturity. He humbly says, "Therefore, gird up the loins of your mind, live soberly, and set your hopes completely on the grace to be brought to you at the revelation of Jesus Christ." Set your hopes completely on Christ. Peter is no longer worried about what he has lost, but rather what he has gained, namely, Christ. In other words, it's not about "mine" or even about "ours," but it's all "yours," meaning Christ's. Peter had reached the heights of holiness and humbly confessed that everything is yours, God's.

Each of us can evaluate our progress on the road of Christian maturity using these three words as our gauge. Where would you say you are on this road? We'd all immediately like to say, "Heck, I'm at the end, in the full blossom of holiness!" That's nice. May I suggest to you that, in reality, we are all pretty much still at the beginning, still worried about what's "mine"? A good tool to use is to pay attention to how often you use the word "I" when you talk to others, when you write, when you think. Or better, notice how others do the same — you'll see that much quicker. The point is, we are often, almost always, self-referential in our conversations, turning the topic onto some personal experience we've had instead of focusing on what the other person is sharing. Watch how often people do that today. Can you walk by a mirror without taking a glance at your appearance? That's a sign the ego is alive and well, perhaps a little too alive. Do you hear humbly and embrace eagerly the constructive criticisms others offer you, or do you feel threatened and become defensive? Do you believe that the whole world is waiting with bated breath to see what you will post next on Facebook? I will give you one guess what I do with my homilies after Masses. Copernicus proved the solar system doesn't revolve around the earth, but we still cling to the hope that the whole world still revolves around us. In other words, maybe it's not just small children who say "Mine!" with quivering lips and a tenacious tug of little hands. We all do, more than we care to admit. We have a long way to go.

PRIDE AND PREJUDICE

Uncovering our hidden biases

•••

MATTHEW 15:21-28

At that time, Jesus withdrew to the region of Tyre and Sidon.

And behold, a Canaanite woman of that district came

and called out, "Have pity on me, Lord, Son of David!

My daughter is tormented by a demon."

But Jesus did not say a word in answer to her.

Jesus' disciples came and asked him,

"Send her away, for she keeps calling out after us."

He said in reply, "I was sent only to the lost sheep of the house

of Israel." But the woman came and did Jesus homage,

saying, "Lord, help me."

He said in reply, "It is not right to take the food of

the children and throw it to the dogs."

She said, "Please, Lord, for even the dogs eat the scraps

that fall from the table of their masters."

Then Jesus said to her in reply, "O woman, great is your faith!

Let it be done for you as you wish."

And the woman's daughter was healed from that hour.

Prejudice comes in all shapes and sizes, and can be found in many famous faces and figures. We quickly recognize the broad strokes of prejudice printed large across the pages of history. For example, the animosity between the North and the South that still rears its ugly head. Some Southerners still speak of the Civil War as "The War of Northern Aggression." Ever heard that one? We see it in the fierce factions and fighting between the Palestinians and the Israelis. These prejudices are plain to everyone. But other forms are more subtle and secret. I recently read the classic *Pride and Prejudice* by Jane Austen, which illustrates how upbringing and environment shape your thinking and sometimes also your prejudices; and you don't know it. Throughout the book, both Lizzy and Mr. Darcy slowly but surely discover their own secret pride and prejudice as they fall in love. By the way, if you'd like to see a musical version of Jane Austen's classic, I recommend the movie *Bride and Prejudice* made by Bollywood in India. It's sure to be a classic!

Shortly after Pope John Paul II died in 2005, I was checking out at a local grocery store. The attendant noticed my Roman collar and said sympathetically, "I was very sad to hear that Pope John Paul II died." And then he added with sincere conviction, "Now, there's one Catholic that's going to heaven!" I replied, "I hope there is room in heaven for two Catholics." Even though that cashier was complimenting the pope, he was still prejudiced toward Catholics, but he didn't recognize it. Sometimes prejudice is easy to spot. But sometimes it is very subtle and secret, hiding in our hearts and hard to see.

In the gospel above, Jesus is helping others to see their hidden prejudices. Jesus speaks alternatively to the disciples and then to the Canaanite woman. Notice that He doesn't grant either party what they request at first. The disciples want Him to dismiss her, but Jesus doesn't. The woman wants a healing, but Jesus doesn't grant it immediately. What is Jesus doing? Just stringing them along? Is He just toying with them? No. He is drawing out their inner prejudices so they can perceive them and so He can heal them. You see, Jesus wants His Jewish disciples to overcome prejudice against non-Jews like the Canaanite woman, and to love her. And He wants the Canaanite woman to see that salvation comes from the Jews, and to love them. In other words, like Lizzy and Mr. Darcy in Austen's book, these gospel characters had grown accustomed to their pride and prejudice, and no longer perceived either as a problem. They didn't see these hidden prejudices.

Someone recently emailed me this joke: An elderly woman died last month. She had never married, and surprisingly, she requested no male pallbearers at her funeral. In her hand-written instructions for her memorial service, she wrote, "They wouldn't take me out while I was alive, and I don't want them to take me out when I am dead." She took revenge from the grave. You could say that poor woman was buried with her bruised pride and prejudice against men.

Have you ever heard of the book *When a Pope Asks Forgiveness,* a collection of the "mea culpas" — saying "I'm sorry" — of Pope John Paul II for sins of the Church over 2,000 years? The sins ranged from the Inquisition to the poor treatment of women. In a touching passage asking forgiveness of women, the pope wrote, "Unfortunately, we are heirs to a history which has conditioned us to a remarkable extent. In every time and place this conditioning has been an obstacle to the progress of women. Women's dignity has often been unacknowledged and their prerogatives misrepresented; they have often been relegated to the margins of society and even reduced to servitude. ..." Then came these beautiful words of humility and hope. He continued, "And if objective blame ... has belonged to not just a few members of the Church, for this I am truly sorry. May this regret be transformed, on the part of the whole Church, into a renewed commitment of fidelity to the Gospel vision." I don't know if John Paul II ever read Jane Austen, but he for one would not let any pride get in the way of a war on prejudice in his own heart and in the heart of the Church. John Paul II wouldn't let prejudice hide anywhere in his heart.

If someone were to ask you, "Are you a racist or a bigot? Do you have prejudices?" how would you respond? We'd all probably answer, "Heck no! I love everyone!" I'm sure that's how the people in the gospel would have answered too. But are you so sure? Because some prejudices are easy to spot, but some are subtle and secret, hiding in our hearts. Here are some masks that prejudice wears when it parades around in public: Some people excuse prejudice when it's disguised as humor. How many jokes have you heard, or perhaps even told, that came at the expense of another person or a class of people? Is racism OK as long as it's funny? Sometimes prejudice wears the mask of fierce patriotism or religious zeal. Around World War II, German Americans changed their German-sounding names to more English-sounding names out of fear of intolerance, hatred and bigotry. The grocery store cashier certainly didn't feel he was being prejudiced against Catholics saying the pope would go to heaven. Another prejudice so subtle that almost no one notices it is what I call "chronological snobbery." It's that sense of superiority and smugness that comes with thinking that whatever is modern is better than whatever is ancient — that just because something is faster and fancier and the fad, it must be better. Now, that may be true when it comes to pancakes and pinball machines, but it is definitely not true when it comes to people. Do you think you are better than your parents? Do you believe you are better than your grandparents? We catch the obvious prejudices people have, but there are many we miss.

In one of my favorite quotations of his, Archbishop Fulton Sheen says, "In heaven there will be three surprises. First, there will be some people there we didn't expect to make it. Second, there will be some people NOT there whom we did expect to make it. And third, the biggest surprise of all is that we ourselves might make it." That grocery store clerk might be surprised at how many Catholics there are in heaven. Who would you be surprised to see in heaven?

THE GIFT OF GAB

Listening and watching more than speaking

•••

ISAIAH 42:1-4

Thus says the LORD:

"Here is my servant whom I uphold,

my chosen one with whom I am pleased,

upon whom I have put my spirit;

he shall bring forth justice to the nations,

not crying out, not shouting,

not making his voice heard in the street.

a bruised reed he shall not break,

and a smoldering wick he shall not quench,

until he establishes justice on the earth;

the coastlands will wait for his teaching."

Do you know where I was before I came to Immaculate Conception? I spent three months in Dallas, Texas, at a Carmelite monastery, to see if God was calling me to a Carmelite monk. Yeah. Believe it or not, I was contemplating becoming a cloistered Carmelite monk. As my niece likes to say, "I know! Right?!" which means, "Are you crazy??" As I was leaving St. Joseph in Fayetteville, Ark., most of the parishioners told me, "Father, you'll never make it as a monk!" I even heard the Las Vegas bookies had given me 1,000–1 odds. Of course, they were all right. I couldn't keep my mouth shut that long; I have the "gift of gab." But the reason I loved the Carmelites was they teach that as prayer grows and deepens, as you try to converse more with Jesus, you need fewer and fewer words. In fact, during the deepest prayer, called contemplation, words just seem to get in the way — they interrupt a more profound conversation carried on between the believer and Jesus, between two hearts. When the heart speaks, it doesn't use words.

Have you ever wondered why God gave us two ears and two eyes, but only one mouth? I believe it's because He wants us to listen with our ears and look with our eyes 80 percent of the time (that's four out of five), but open our big mouths only 20 percent of the time (that's one out of five). But what normally happens? It's usually the opposite, isn't it? That's the old pareto principle at work — 20 percent of the people always do 80 percent of the work. Our mouths are way too busy! We even talk too much in prayer, and listen and watch way too little. So, that's why I became pastor of Immaculate Conception Church: because I can't keep my mouth shut. That's not necessarily a bad thing — indeed the gift of gab is a good thing — but there's something even better: listening and watching, which we should do far more than talking.

In the verses above, Isaiah prophesies that this will be the hallmark of the Messiah: He'll use His eyes and His ears far more than His mouth. Listen now to Isaiah: "Here is my servant whom I uphold ... he shall bring forth justice to the nations, not crying out, not shouting, not making his voice heard in the street." And then Isaiah's imagery grows more tender. He says, "A bruised reed he shall not break, and a smoldering wick he shall not quench." In other words, the Messiah will not have the gift of gab! Instead, His eyes and ears — and most especially His heart — will be open to the plight of the poor and lowly.

His watchful eyes will see the bruised reed and not break it; His sharp ears will hear the smoldering wick and not quench it. You won't be able to apply the pareto principle to the Messiah: His mouth will only do 20 percent of the work because, sometimes, words just get in the way.

Can I tell you something that really bugs me about Jesus? I hope this doesn't sound irreverent, but I gotta know: Why on earth did Jesus decide to come to earth 2,000 years ago instead of today? Just think of all the technological limitations of the first century that we don't have: no decent roads, primitive water supply, unreliable communication, and they didn't even have cell phones. And there's plenty of confusion surrounding the Scriptures, too. For instance, we're not sure what language Jesus spoke to the apostles — maybe it was Hebrew, or perhaps Aramaic, or maybe even Greek. Since we don't know what language He used, we don't really know exactly what words He said. Many scholars even dispute and debate if Jesus actually said some of the words attributed to Him in the Gospels. For instance, maybe Matthew "ad-libbed" or John took poetic liberties in that long Last Supper discourse. There's no way to know for sure. But if Jesus had lived today, it would have been so easy! Jesus could write His own book, and you could download it and listen to our Lord's podcast on your morning jog. Jesus could post His latest sermon on Facebook, and see how many "likes" and "shares" He gets. Jesus could tweet a parable-a-day to all His "followers." Jesus could take a selfie after a miracle and post it on Instagram. It would be great if Jesus had come now! So, why didn't He?

Well, frankly, I don't know. But here's my best guess: The Messiah wasn't worried that much about words, and He didn't care much about the gift of gab. Instead, He came to listen and to see, to communicate something deeper than words can capture; to invite us into a conversation that texts and tweets and tumblrs actually create an obstacle for, a dialogue between two hearts. As your friendship with Jesus grows and deepens, words actually begin to get in the way. St. John Vianney, the

Cure of Ars and patron saint of parish priests, used this borrowed quote to describe how he prayed: "I love to go into the empty church at night, and sit down in front of the Blessed Sacrament. I look at Jesus, and he looks at me." What a great description of prayer: "I look at Jesus and he looks at me." When the heart speaks, it doesn't need to use words.

Using your eyes and ears rather than your mouth, listening and seeing instead of speaking excessively, will benefit your human relationships, too. I love to hear about families that still sit down for supper and truly share a meal together — and no cell phones allowed at the table! They look at each other, listen to each other, sincerely pay attention to what others say, and talk less. I wonder if this is why so many people seek therapy from professional counselors. During those therapy sessions, we know that counselor will give us their undivided and complete attention — something we rarely get from other people — and they will mostly use their eyes and their ears, and only sparingly use their mouths. When I used to see older couples sitting in restaurants eating their meals and hardly speaking to each other, I thought, "Wow, how sad. They don't have anything to say to each other. They must not love each other anymore." But maybe I wasn't seeing the whole picture. Maybe they were carrying on a conversation that didn't need words, where just a look or a smile, a frown or a cough, were more eloquent that Emily Dickenson's poems and sweeter than Shakespeare's sonnets. When hearts speak, words sometimes get in the way.

My friends, do you have the gift of gab like I do? Let me give you a little advice. First of all, don't go join the Carmelites; they will kick you out in three months. Second, look in the mirror every day and ask yourself, "Why did God give me two eyes and two ears and only one mouth?" As my niece likes to say: "I know! Right?!"

THE IMPOSSIBLE DREAM OF MARRIAGE

Leaning on Jesus to enjoy a lifelong marriage

•••

Daniel 3:19-20, 91-92, 95

King Nebuchadnezzar's face became livid with

utter rage against Shadrach, Meshach, and Abednego.

He ordered the furnace to be heated seven times more

than usual and had some of the strongest men in his

army bind Shadrach, Meshach, and Abednego and

cast them into the white-hot furnace. Nebuchadnezzar

rose in haste and asked his nobles,

"Did we not cast three men bound into the fire?"

"Assuredly, O king," they answered.

"But," he replied, "I see four men unfettered and unhurt,

walking in the fire, and the fourth looks like a son of God."

Nebuchadnezzar exclaimed,

"Blessed be the God of Shadrach, Meshach, and Abednego,

who sent his angel to deliver the servants

who trusted in him;

they disobeyed the royal command and yielded

their bodies rather than serve or worship any god

except their own God."

I believe that every man and woman who has ever married attempts to do something superhuman. Every husband is Superman and every wife is Wonder Woman. Why? I am convinced that to stay married to one person for the whole of your life is humanly impossible. Why do you think I became a priest? We think priests do something really hard — remain celibate — but that's relatively easy compared to the commitment of marriage. When I talk to young engaged couples, I tell them that no matter how much love, kindness and patience you feel today, the day will come when you'll feel you cannot go on, that you don't have an ounce of love left. On that day, you'll have to do something superhuman. I urge them to lean on Jesus and He will give them the grace to do the impossible. What is the secret to a lifelong marriage? The secret is Jesus.

In the passage above, three men do the impossible, but only with God's help. Shadrach, Meshach and Abednego are thrown into a fiery furnace, and they walk on coals and even sing songs. To me, the superhuman part is the singing: to sing while you suffer. When King Nebuchadnezzar peered into the furnace, he didn't see three men, but four, and the fourth looked like a son of God. That fourth person was a pre-figuration of Jesus. The secret of being Superman and Wonder Woman is walking in the company of Jesus.

One of my favorite Broadway musicals is *The Man of La Mancha*. Don Quixote sings this stirring song explaining his impossible quest called *The Impossible Dream*. Every couple married for more than five months has wanted to sing it, too, about their own marriage. It goes:

To dream ... the impossible dream ...
To fight ... the unbeatable foe ...
To bear ... the unbearable sorrow ...
To run ... where the brave dare not go ...
To right ... the unrightable wrong ...

To love ... pure and chaste from afar ...
To try ... when your arms are too weary ...
To reach ... the unreachable star ...

The secret strength to be able to sing when you are suffering comes from Christ. Only with Jesus can you dare to dream the impossible dream called marriage.

THE MIDDLE MATTERS
Making the most of our earthly life

• • •

LUKE 21:5-19

While some people were speaking about how the temple was
adorned with costly stones and votive offerings, Jesus said,
"All that you see here — the days will come when there will not
be left a stone upon another stone that will not be thrown down."
Then they asked him, "Teacher, when will this happen?
And what sign will there be when all these things
are about to happen?"
He answered, "See that you not be deceived, for many will come
in my name, saying, 'I am he,' and 'The time has come.'
Do not follow them! When you hear of wars and insurrections,
do not be terrified; for such things must happen first,
but it will not immediately be the end."
Then he said to them, "Nation will rise against nation,
and kingdom against kingdom. There will be powerful
earthquakes, famines, and plagues from place to place;
and awesome sights and mighty signs will come from the sky.
Before all this happens, however, they will seize and
persecute you, they will hand you over to the synagogues

and to prisons, and they will have you led before

kings and governors because of my name.

It will lead to your giving testimony.

Remember, you are not to prepare your defense beforehand,

for I myself shall give you a wisdom in speaking that all your

adversaries will be powerless to resist or refute.

You will even be handed over by parents, brothers, relatives, and

friends, and they will put some of you to death.

You will be hated by all because of my name, but not a hair

on your head will be destroyed.

By your perseverance you will secure your lives."

Every story has a beginning, a middle and an end. They taught us that in high school composition class, when we first started writing serious papers. The beginning introduces the theme or the main characters, the middle unfolds the plot, and the end ties it all together and draws a conclusion or a moral lesson. In the seminary, they taught us that a good homily or sermon also has a beginning, a middle and an end. Now, George Burns, the great comedian, once said, "The secret of a good sermon is to have a good beginning, and a good end, then having the two as close together as possible." You might recall that George Burns played God in a movie, so we should take his advice very seriously. But with all due respect to Mr. Burns, the middle also matters. The middle of the story is where the plot thickens, where the characters interact, where either virtue or vice triumph, where the substance of the argument is presented, which either convinces or fails to persuade. Omitting the middle would be like going to a fine restaurant and ordering the appetizer, skipping the entrée and going straight to dessert. Sorry, Mr. Burns, but the middle matters.

While stories and sermons have a beginning, a middle and an end, so do the histories of our lives. Think about this: Each person is right in the middle of the story of your life — some are closer to the end than others. Your tombstone will only record the date of your birth and the date of your death, but everything that happens in between those dates matters, too. Have you ever heard how Leonardo DaVinci chose the faces for his famous painting of the Last Supper? One Sunday, as DaVinci was at the cathedral for Mass, he saw a young man in the choir who looked like DaVinci's idea of how Jesus must have looked. He had the features of love, tenderness, caring, innocence and kindness. Arrangements were made for the young man, Pietri Bandinelli, to sit as a model for the Lord. However, DaVinci couldn't find just the right face for Judas. He was looking for a man whose face was streaked with despair, wickedness, greed and sin. Ten years after starting the painting, he found a man in prison whose face wore all the qualities of Judas for which he has been searching. Consent was given for the prisoner to pose as the model for Judas. As Leonardo worked, he noticed the prisoner was tense and agitated, and finally the artist asked him what was wrong. The prisoner buried his face in his hands, and between sobs of despair, said, "Don't you remember me? Years ago I was your model for the Lord, Jesus." The same face that seemed to be the very promise of Paradise had crumbled into the depths of despair. What happens in the middle matters.

In the gospel above, Jesus is speaking about the end of the world, which will be characterized by wars, insurrections, earthquakes and famine. But that's not really Jesus' main point. What He really wants His disciples to do is to pay attention to their lives now — the intervening years — how they will give testimony by their example, how they will speak with a wisdom Jesus will give, how they will persevere in the face of great opposition even from family members. In other words, Jesus cautions them, don't be so laser focused on the end that you don't worry about the middle. The middle matters. It matters a great deal. Don't be hedonistic and, raising a glass, say, "Let's eat, drink and be merry, for tomorrow we die!" as if how we live right now doesn't amount to much or has no future consequences. What we do before we die, how we live until the end of the world, matters a great deal, too. Like those two main characters in DaVinci's Last Supper, our choices are making our faces either more like that of Jesus, or more like that of Judas. You see, it's the middle that matters.

My story, too, is in the middle chapters, beginning in New Delhi, India, through St. Joseph in Fayetteville, Ark., and now at Immaculate Conception Church in Ft. Smith, Ark. The history of each of these parishes has intersected with my own. And all of our stories will march on until the Lord returns in glory. We meet each other in the middle of our lives, and how we interact, how we love one another (or fail to love one another), how we bring one another closer to Christ (or push one another away from Him), is not a small thing! The middle matters.

A friend once described how we touch each other's lives with this metaphor: Imagine a brick made of solid gold and another brick of solid silver. If you pressed those two bricks against each other hard, and held them together for years, when you finally pulled them apart, there would be some gold specks embedded in the silver brick and some silver specks embedded in the gold brick. However long we are together, you will leave some specks of you on me, and I will leave some specks on you. Don't just worry about the end — some may already be wondering, "When is this guy going to leave?" or "When is this sermon going to end?" — but rather about the middle. Don't wish for your relationships to just end, even if it's a marriage headed toward a divorce. If you're elderly, don't long for your life to come to an end, even if you're terminally ill. If you're a teenager, don't rush to get out of the house as soon as possible. What happens in the middle matters — how we touch each other's lives and bless each other, or fail to. May my pastorate be a blessing to you, and may each parishioner be a blessing to me.

Do you remember how Dante's masterpiece *The Divine Comedy* begins? The opening line reads, "In the middle of the journey of our lives, I found myself within a dark wood where the straight way was lost." And then Dante begins his journey into hell with the help of Virgil, a friend sent from heaven. The whole *Divine Comedy* is really a story about how the middle matters; what happened to Dante in the middle of his life. You and I, too, will lean on each other to find the straight way when it is lost. I'll try not to make it hell for you, if you'll try not to make it hell for me. With the help of Virgil, and later aided by Beatrice, Dante eventually makes it to heaven. You and I will do the same for each other, leaning on each other and helping each other take a few steps closer to heaven, a few steps closer to Christ. Because you see, what happens in the middle is ultimately what matters.

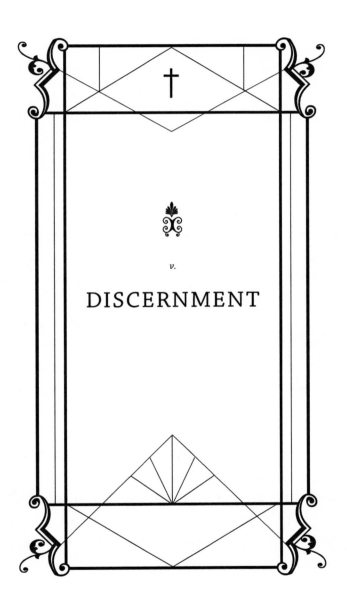

v.

DISCERNMENT

Have you ever thrust a stick into a pool of water and noticed anything peculiar? The submerged portion of the stick will appear bent below the surface of the water. If you plunge your hand into the water to feel the stick, immediately you'll discover that your eyes deceived you and the stick is not bent at all. The sense of touch helps correct your sense of sight. This is an example of discernment. What at first sight seemed clear and obvious turned out to be otherwise, upon further inspection and cross-examination. Discernment, then, is a process of scrutinizing the reality of things until we can, little by little, begin to see things as they truly are.

All successful discernment begins with a healthy suspicion of how we see things. We first humbly confess: Perhaps the stick below the water is not bent after all, even though it's obvious to me that it is. This healthy suspicion is captured by maxims such as "not all that glitters is gold" and "do not judge a book by its cover." If you refuse to accept this suspicion, that possibility that perhaps you don't know everything, then all future discernment will be futile. Writer and theologian G. K. Chesterton expressed the spirit of such a stubborn person, saying, "There are no uninteresting things; there are only uninterested people." A little self-effacing interest — that healthy and holy suspicion that maybe I have more to learn — sparks the great adventure of discernment.

No one can help us see the truth of things better than Jesus Himself. Humbly declaring Himself the lodestar of all discernment, our Lord said, "I am the way, the truth and the life. No one comes to the Father except through me" (John 14:6). Jesus is literally truth on two legs. The Second Vatican Council affirmed this same teaching: "Jesus Christ, the new Adam, fully reveals man to himself and makes his supreme calling clear" (Gaudium et spes, 22). In other words, once we see ourselves and the world through the eyes of Christ, once He corrects all our human errors and misperceptions, we glimpse the full truth of things, with no need of further cross-examination. If discernment commences with a healthy suspicion that I don't see straight, it concludes with the confidence that now I see all things through the eyes of Jesus.

Every homily in this chapter is concerned with taking a step toward that comprehensive vision of faith, to see as Jesus sees. "Sirach's Compass" keeps us oriented to Christ when life's complexity causes us to wander. "Twenty Minutes of Hell" helps us manage our expectations about life more in line with God's hopes for us. "O, Dark Thirty" reminds us that it is in the darkness that Christ's light shines brightest. And "Feminine Genius" shows that women grasp God's goodness and grace precisely so they can share it with the world. Let me invite you to read each homily as a conversation with Christ: Begin with that healthy suspicion of your own limited knowledge, and end by peering at the world through Jesus' eyes. Perhaps you'll perceive what Paul did when he said with profound confidence, "For everything belongs to you, and you belong to Christ, and Christ belongs to God" (1 Corinthians 3:23).

ALL ABOARD FOR HEAVEN

Giving up earthly things in order to enter heaven

•••

Matthew 6:24-34

Jesus said to his disciples: "No one can serve two masters.

He will either hate one and love the other, or be devoted to one

and despise the other. You cannot serve God and mammon.

"Therefore I tell you, do not worry about your life, what you will

eat or drink, or about your body, what you will wear.

Is not life more than food and the body more than clothing?

Look at the birds in the sky; they do not sow or reap, they gather

nothing into barns, yet your heavenly Father feeds them.

Are not you more important than they? Can any of you by

worrying add a single moment to your life-span?

Why are you anxious about clothes? Learn from the way the wild

flowers grow. They do not work or spin. But I tell you that not

even Solomon in all his splendor was clothed like one of them.

If God so clothes the grass of the field, which grows today and is

thrown into the oven tomorrow, will he not much more provide

for you, O you of little faith? So do not worry and say,

'What are we to eat?' or 'What are we to drink?'

or 'What are we to wear?'

All these things the pagans seek.

Your heavenly Father knows that you need them all.

But seek first the kingdom of God and his righteousness,

and all these things will be given you besides.

Do not worry about tomorrow; tomorrow will take care of itself.

Sufficient for a day is its own evil."

My favorite book by C.S. Lewis is one that very few people have heard of and even fewer people have read: *The Great Divorce*. After all, who wants to read about a divorce, even if it is a "great" one? It doesn't really have anything to do with marriage and divorce, but rather, it's about an imaginary bus trip to heaven and Lewis' startling claim that you can't take any souvenirs from earth into heaven. Here's how he puts it: "You cannot take all luggage with you on all journeys; on one journey (here he means to heaven) even your right hand and your right eye may be among the things you leave behind." Remember in the Bible where Jesus says that if your right hand causes you to sin, cut it off, and if your right eye causes you to sin, tear it out? Lewis continues: "If we insist on keeping earth, we shall not see Heaven; if we accept Heaven we shall not be able to retain even the smallest souvenirs of earth." For just a moment, try to visualize packing your suitcase for a trip to heaven. What would you take? Would you take your favorite teddy bear, pack your jogging shoes, charge your Kindle and download books, throw in plenty of sunscreen? Or, put another way, what would you want to have in heaven so much that, without it, it wouldn't feel much like heaven?

Several years ago, there was a news story about a man who loved his Cadillac so much that when he died, he wanted to be buried with it, with his body placed in the driver's seat. He said he wanted to drive his Caddy in heaven. That's a true story; you can't make this stuff up. Two friends were discussing the passing of a very wealthy neighbor. One asked, "How much did he leave behind?" The other answered, "He left it all behind." That's what C.S. Lewis was asserting: We won't take anything material with us to heaven. Do you recall that famous line from the Old Testament book of Job, where Job exclaimed, "Naked I came forth from my mother's womb; naked I will return there" (Job 1:21)? When we return to heaven, we'll all go back in our birthday suits.

Now, here's the hard thing to understand about heaven: It won't be simply a continuation of life as we know it on earth — more of the same but just a lot better. That's what most people expect heaven to be like, but it won't. Rather, there will be a radical break with earthly life, a dramatic departure, for which Lewis decided to use the drastic term "the great divorce." Grasping that dramatic difference between heaven and earth is the hard part of heaven.

In the gospel above, Jesus is trying to prepare His disciples for that final bus trip to heaven, so that, when they climb aboard that heaven-bound bus, they can leave behind all their luggage. Our Lord says rather starkly: "No one can serve two masters. He will either hate one and love the other, or be devoted to one and despise the other. You cannot serve God and mammon." That is, they cannot love both heaven and earth equally; they must choose one, they must love one decisively more than they love the other. When Jesus uses the term "mammon," He's referring to all the things they'd like to pack on that bus trip to heaven; the things they feel they just could not live without. That's why Jesus goes on to list the things they tended to worry overmuch about (really, to love too much): security, food, clothing. But His point is clear, even if uncomfortable: You cannot pack anything for heaven. The apostles must love God more than they love their teddy bear, more than they love their Cadillac, more than they love their chai latte.

Have you decided what you'll give up for Lent this year? Now, don't be like one of my friends who always waits until the end of Lent and asks himself, "Let's see, what did I NOT eat or drink for the past 40 days? That's my Lenten sacrifice!" Sorry, there are no "retroactive Lenten penances." Maybe you'll adopt the attitude of one of our second graders who said, "I'm going to give up watching six minutes of TV every day!" Hey, that's a big sacrifice for some people! May I suggest another way to look at Lent? Try to think ahead to that inevitable bus trip you'll take one day to heaven. What are the things you think you cannot live without in heaven: your morning coffee and newspaper, your favorite playlist of songs, texting, tweeting and Facebook, watching *American Idol* and drinking a cold Coors Light? Give up these things for Lent; you'll have to give them up one day.

Now, don't misunderstand me: We don't give these things up because they are bad; indeed, they are good things. God made them for our happiness. Rather, we give them up because sacrificing them shows we love God more than these things. You see, Lent is a kind of litmus test of love to see if you really do "love God more than mammon." It's so easy to say, "Yeah, I love God!" It's a lot harder to show it.

Then, if we truly love God more than mammon during Lent, something beautiful will happen at Easter. We will celebrate the Resurrection. And I don't just mean Jesus' Resurrection, but, in a spiritual sense, also our own Resurrection. Just as Jesus had to be stripped of everything of this world — all the worldly mammon — during His passion and death so that He could rise on the third day, so must we. The cost of that bus ride to heaven is the same for everyone, including Jesus: We must leave behind all our luggage. You could say that every Lent and Easter we are invited to take a little "day trip" to heaven. But like before any vacation, the hard part is knowing what to pack and what to leave behind. That's what you have to figure out every Lent: What is one more thing you must learn to leave behind before you can board that bus? "You cannot take all luggage with you on all journeys; on one journey even your right hand and your right eye may be among the things you have to leave behind."

APPLES AND PAIRS

Trusting in God for our happiness

•••

Matthew 7:7-12

Jesus said to his disciples: "Ask and it will be given to you;
seek and you will find; knock and the door will be opened to you.
For everyone who asks, receives; and the one who seeks, finds;
and to the one who knocks, the door will be opened.
Which one of you would hand his son a stone when he asked for
a loaf of bread, or a snake when he asked for a fish?
If you then, who are wicked, know how to give good gifts
to your children, how much more will your heavenly Father
give good things to those who ask him.
Do to others whatever you would have them do to you.
This is the law and the prophets."

Pope John Paul II gave me a whole new way of understanding the Adam and Eve story, especially the sin of eating the apple. Most Scripture commentators say the first couple committed an act of disobedience, and that's true. They violated God's express prohibition not to eat of the forbidden fruit. Other commentators say it was pride and arrogance, wanting to be like God themselves. After all, wasn't this precisely what the diabolic Serpent promised them? Scripture scholar Scott Hahn suggested that it was a sexual sin. He joked, "The problem was not the apple on the tree, but the pair on the ground." Get it: not an apple but a pear! John Paul II, however, said what lay at the root of their sin was a lack of trust. You see, God had built the whole Garden of Eden, saying in effect: "I have provided all this for your happiness. You can trust me to take care of you." But Adam and Eve said, "Thanks, but no thanks. We'll trust someone else to make us happy; we'll trust the Serpent." And the rest is history: the history of a humanity that fails again and again to trust in the Father's love. All of human history can be seen through this lens — a timeless tale of committing the same sin of Adam and Eve, and failure to trust God for our happiness. We are truly children of our first parents. You could say the apple didn't fall far from the tree.

This is how we should understand the gospel passage above: in the context of reestablishing that broken trust in the Father. Jesus says, "Which one of you would hand his son a stone when he asked for a loaf of bread, or a snake when he asked for a fish? If you then, who are wicked, know how to give good gifts to your children, how much more will your heavenly Father give good things to those who ask him." Every mother's and every father's heart beats with one overriding impulse: to give their children the best. In fact, most parents want their children to have far better than they had themselves. Every mother and father says in effect to their children, "Trust me, I'll take care of you. I truly want your happiness." But sooner or later, most children repeat the fatal words of Adam and Eve: "Thanks, but no thanks. I'll trust someone else to make me happy." But Jesus shows us another way, and it's the road of total trust in God. Jesus not only taught us how to trust the Father, but He also modeled how to do it, all the way to the Cross. That's what Adam and Eve should have done: put their total trust in God.

Do you truly trust God? I really believe this is the most important thing we have to do. Here's another way to look at it: Every sin is at root a statement of lack of trust in God. If we truly trusted God, we would pull the rug out from under every desire to sin; we would be exactly like Jesus, who trusted totally. Behind every sin is a lack of trust in God. Behind every adulterous affair, behind every South American drug cartel, behind every mother's gambling addiction, behind every priest's excessive drinking, behind every student who cheats on a test, behind every masked bank robber, behind every Mass we skip on Sunday, behind every word of gossip, behind every white or black lie, behind every ruthless dictator lies one final and fundamental fact: We don't trust God for our happiness. We say with every sin, "Thanks but no thanks. I'll trust something or someone else to make me happy." Even our money reminds us that it's "In God we trust." But do we? Adam and Eve's sin had little to do with apples and pairs, but everything to do with a lack of trust. It's the same for each of our sins: Ultimately, they're the result of a failure to trust in the Father's love. If we totally trusted God, we wouldn't sin.

Adam and Eve's mistake has traditionally been called "The Original Sin" because every sin since then has just been a knockoff. The apple didn't fall far from the original tree.

FEMININE GENIUS

Grasping the fundamental law of love

•••

JOHN 15:9-17

Jesus said to his disciples: "As the Father loves me,
so I also love you. Remain in my love. If you keep my
commandments, you will remain in my love, just as I have kept
my Father's commandments and remain in his love."
"I have told you this so that my joy may be in you and your joy
might be complete. This is my commandment: love one another
as I love you. No one has greater love than this, to lay down
one's life for one's friends. You are my friends if you do what
I command you. I no longer call you slaves, because a slave does
not know what his master is doing. I have called you friends,
because I have told you everything I have heard from my Father.
It was not you who chose me, but I who chose you and appointed
you to go and bear fruit that will remain, so that whatever you
ask the Father in my name he may give you.
This I command you: love one another."

God is smart. I don't know if you've noticed that before, but I perceived
His divine genius in a profound way this past week. Recently, my sister-

in-law brought her two daughters, my young nieces, to the rectory so I could drive them to school. Before we left the house, we cuddled on the couch and they told me their plans for the day. I can't tell you how good it felt just to hold my nieces in my arms, and they obviously didn't mind either. In a flash, I saw how smart God is. He made us to love each other; you could say He hardwired us that way. Here's what I realized sitting on the couch holding my nieces: God made adults with a need to hug children — we love to hold them — and He made children with a need to be hugged by adults — they love to be held. Adults and children are perfectly suited for each other, each fulfilling the other's instinctive needs for love and affection. Isn't that genius? Leadership guru Stephen Covey calls that a "win-win." God designed a hug so that adults win and children win.

Now what I caught at a passing glance, I think that women, especially mothers, perceive and feel all the time. And you ladies who are moms don't just feel this all the time, but you feel it a thousand times more intensely than I — a celibate, single, childless priest — ever could. In other words, a woman's maternal instinct alerts her intuitively to this basic law of love — how a hug works, mutually benefitting both parties — designed by God himself. Women easily identify God's genius woven into the fabric of relationships, while it took this Catholic priest 42 years and two graduate degrees to finally figure it out.

Pope John Paul II described this sacred sensitivity, a woman's awareness of God's plan of love, as "feminine genius." I love that phrase: feminine genius. Listen to the pope's admiration for women in his Apostolic Letter on the role and vocation of women, in Latin titled *Mulieris Dignitatem.* He writes: "The success of science and technology make it possible to attain material well-being to a degree hitherto unknown. While this favors some, it pushes others to the edges of society. In this way, unilateral progress can also lead to a gradual loss of sensitivity for man, that is, what is essentially human. In this sense, our time in particular awaits the manifestation of that 'genius' which belongs to women, and which can ensure sensitivity for human beings in every circumstance." In other words, the pope fully agrees that I'm not the only clueless male in the world! Many men and even women don't grasp the basic law of mutual love and affection that should guide human relationships. Without the special sensitivity of women, the relentless march of science and technology would eradicate what is essentially human from the world. In a sense, the whole world is eagerly waiting for women to unleash their "feminine genius" to show us God's plan of love: that we are made to love each other. That divine plan of love is hidden in something as simple as a hug.

In the gospel above, Jesus tries to teach His apostles this law of love in multiple ways. First, He says my Father and I love each other. That is, love is the native language of heaven, how the Father and the Son communicate. Then He says that keeping His commandments is proof of love. Jesus doesn't say, "Show me the money!" He says, "Show me the love!" To sweeten the pot a little more, He adds that loving each other will bring you complete joy. Moreover, Jesus explains that the apostles will be His friends if they love each other. Finally, our Lord says if you love each other, you will bear great fruit. Jesus is saying in effect, "Look, how many different ways do I have to tell you to love each other?!" But the apostles were a lot like me and like most men and even some women — slow and stubborn — and they wouldn't really "get" the law of love until the Holy Spirit descended at Pentecost. On the other hand, the women, like Mary, got it from the get-go, with the help of their feminine genius. Those first female disciples, as well as women up and down the generations, can detect the eternal law of love snuggled in something as simple as a hug.

One day in the Garden of Eden, Eve is talking to God. She says, "Lord, I have a problem." God asks, "What is it, Eve?" She says, "Lord, I know you created me and provided this beautiful garden and all of these wonderful animals, but I'm lonely." God says, "Well, Eve, in that case I have a solution. I'll create a man for you." Eve asks, "What is a man?" God answers, "This man will be a flawed creature, with aggressive tendencies, an enormous ego, an inability to empathize or listen to you properly. But he'll be bigger and faster and more muscular than you. He'll really be good at fighting and kicking a ball and hunting animals." Eve says, "Sounds great," but a little suspicious, she adds, "What's the catch?" God says, "Well, you can have him on one condition." Eve asks, "What's that?" God explains, "Well, as I said, he'll be proud and egotistical, so you'll have to let him believe that I created him first." If you didn't get that joke, ask a woman sitting close to you; she'll be happy to explain. Now, that's a whole different kind of feminine genius! The feminine genius that John Paul II espouses, on the other hand, clues us into God's genius: He made us to love each other.

In every woman called to be a mother, the feminine genius reaches its zenith, its apex, its high point. On Mother's Day, I always want to say two things to our moms and to my mom in particular. First of all, "Thank you!" Thank you, Mom, for the gift of life, for carrying me in your womb and loving me for nine months before I ever saw the light of day. Thank you for enduring all the morning sickness, the back pain, the sleepless nights, the exhaustion, the pickles and ice cream, and, finally, the excruciating pain of labor. You know, whenever I think I'm hot stuff for running a marathon, a good friend quickly reminds me that a woman who's had a baby can run circles around a marathoner. So, thanks, Mom.

Second, moms, please don't forget or forfeit your feminine genius; and especially don't try to be like us men. Of course, I'm not suggesting that women should get out of the workplace, or that women should not be in politics, or that women shouldn't contribute to science, or the arts, or even in the Church. What I do mean, however, is that I pray you women won't lose touch with your feminine genius, that unique grasp of God's law of love which only you have, and which the world desperately needs. Because you see, at the end of the day, how we're supposed to relate to each other is not defined by entrepreneurial capitalism, or by partisan politics, or by class-warfare communism, or by majority-vote democracy, or by socialism, or by fascism or by anything else. We're supposed to love each other; that should be the root of each and every one of our relationships. The feminine genius is the key to unlock God's own genius: that He created us to love and be loved.

I hope you cook up some creative gifts for your mom this next Mother's Day. I hope you give her cards and balloons and chocolates and take her to a fancy restaurant. In addition to all that, I also hope you give your mom a long, tender hug. You see, mothers, like small children, also like to be held and hugged. And you won't have to explain why you're doing that, because, you see, your mom is a genius.

MARY DID KNOW

Seeing the world through a mother's eyes

• • •

LUKE 2:16-21

The shepherds went in haste to Bethlehem and found
Mary and Joseph, and the infant lying in the manger.
When they saw this, they made known the message that had
been told them about this child.
All who heard it were amazed by what had been told them
by the shepherds. And Mary kept all these things,
reflecting on them in her heart. Then the shepherds returned,
glorifying and praising God for all they had heard and seen,
just as it had been told to them. When eight days were
completed for his circumcision, he was named Jesus,
the name given him by the angel before he was
conceived in the womb.

No one knows their children better than their mothers. Sorry, dads, even more than you. And I don't mean because mothers enjoy some vague sense of woman's intuition; they know them better than that. This knowing their child begins all the way back at conception and lasts for nine months before the baby makes his or her debut. But even after the umbilical cord is cut, the baby and mother are virtually insep-arable. Listen to these insightful lines from theologian Scott Hahn's book on the motherhood of Mary, *Hail, Holy Queen.* Hahn writes, "Perhaps motherhood is so little understood and appreciated because our mothers are so close to us. Infants, for example, don't even under-stand that Mother is a separate entity until they are several months old. Some researchers say that children don't fully come to this realization until they are weaned." A few pages later he adds, "After birth, nature places the child at the mother's breast for nourishment. The newborn's eyes can see only far enough to make eye contact with Mom." All this contact and communion puts mom in the perfect position not only to observe her baby, but also to know her baby better than anyone else.

This past week, I saw my own mother and she was reminiscing about my childhood. She said, "You know, you cried all the time: You cried at home, you cried in school, you cried in church." I asked, "Well, Mom, isn't there anything else you recall?" She answered, "No, that's pretty much all there is to remember." As kids say these days, "Wow, Mom!" You see, no one knows you as well as your mother.

In the gospel above, we hear how Mary flexed the muscles of her maternal memory to record every detail of Jesus' birth. She knew Him better than anyone else. Luke describes the arrival of the shepherds, but then adds, "And Mary kept all these things, reflecting on them in her heart." But Mary did more than reminisce over the past like my mom remembered my crying. Mary prayed as she pondered. When you pray, you see things through God's eyes, and you almost begin to know things like God knows things. Have you heard that popular Christian song *Mary, Did You Know?* One verse goes, "Mary, did you know that your Baby Boy will give sight to a blind man? Mary did you know that your Baby Boy will calm the storm with His hand? Did you know that your Baby Boy has walked where angels trod, When you kiss your little Baby, you kissed the face of God?" The song asks a rhetorical question, and the obvious answer is, "Well, no, Mary did not know all these things. How could she?" But I disagree; I think she did know. Why? Because no one knows their child like a mother does, and our Mother Mary is no ordinary multitasking, soccer mom — she's the Mother of God, preserved from sin since her conception. And what's more, when she pondered she also prayed. When you pray, you see the world like God sees it, not through rose-colored glasses, but through grace-colored glasses. Anyone who has prayed seriously has caught glimpses of this vision of the world, where all is grace and everything is a gift. That's how Mary saw the world, and that's exactly how Mary saw Jesus, as a total gift. Yes, Mary knew a lot about Jesus.

Now, this motherly Mensa club Mary is the head of is not just highfalutin theology for priests and seminary professors. It's very practical and useful for today's mom. For example, after a recent Mass, I overheard how one mother got her fidgety 7-year-old boy to sit still and be quiet. About halfway through the sermon, during the second verse of "Grandma Got Run Over by a Reindeer," she leaned over and whispered, "If you don't be quiet, Father will lose his place and will have to start his sermon all over again!" Worked like a charm because moms know their children. Children also feel free to share everything with their mothers. One young boy happily announced one Sunday to his mother, "Mom, I've decided to become a priest when I grow up." She answered, "That's OK with us, but what made you decide that?" "Well," said the little boy, "I have to go to church on Sunday anyway, and I figure it will be more fun to stand up and yell than to sit down and listen." So, all moms know their children, but no mom knows their child like Mary knew Jesus.

Every January 1 we celebrate the Feast of Mary, the Mother of God. But she's not just the Mother of God; she's also our mother. So, let me ask you: Do you look at Mary as your mother? Do you relate to her as Mom? A great way to do that is to pray the Rosary meditatively. How about that for a New Year's resolution: Pray the Rosary devoutly every day, or at least once a week. More than just adding another item to your spiritual to-do list, however, something beautiful happens when you pray the Rosary, when you get closer to your mother Mary. You not only get to know Mary better, but you also get to know yourself better. Why? Because no one knows their children like their mother, and you'll begin to know yourself like she knows you. There is a small but striking detail in the image of Our Lady of Guadalupe. Through microscopic analysis, they've found that in the pupil of her eye is reflected a perfect image of St. Juan Diego, to whom she appeared. That's where that tender saying "You're the apple of my eye" comes from. In other words, Mary didn't just come to tell Juan Diego who Jesus is; she came to tell Juan Diego who Juan Diego is! Mary can do that for him and for us better than anyone else. Why? Because no one knows their child like their mother. If you want to know who Jesus is, and you want to know who you are, ask your mother Mary. The rosary will help you get close enough so you can see your reflection in her loving eyes, like an infant at the breast.

Let me conclude with Archbishop Fulton Sheen's favorite poem about Mary; it's my favorite, too. It goes:

Lovely Lady, dressed in blue.
Teach me how to pray!
God was just your little boy,
Tell me what to say.
Did you lift Him up sometimes,
Gently on your knee?
Did you sing to Him the way,
Mother does to me?
Did you hold His hand at night?
Did you ever try,

Telling Him stories of the world?
O! and did He cry?
Do you really think He cares,
If I tell Him things,
Little things that happen?
And do angels' wings make a noise?
And can He hear me if I speak low?
Does He hear me now?
Tell me — for you know.
Lovely Lady dressed in blue —
Teach me how to pray!
God was just your little boy,
and you know the way.

Yes, Mary knows.

O, DARK THIRTY

Enjoying the light while walking in the dark

•••

ISAIAH 9:1-3

The people who walked in darkness have seen a great light;
upon those who dwelt in the land of gloom a light has shone.
You have brought them abundant joy and great rejoicing, as they
rejoice before you as at the harvest, as people make merry
when dividing spoils. For the yoke that burdened them, the pole
on their shoulder, and the rod of their taskmaster you have
smashed, as on the day of Midian.

LUKE 2:8-14

Now there were shepherds in that region
living in the fields and keeping the night watch over their flock.
The angel of the Lord appeared to them and the glory of the Lord
shone around them, and they were struck with great fear.
The angel said to them, "Do not be afraid; for behold, I proclaim
to you good news of great joy that will be for all the people.
For today in the city of David a savior has been born for you
who is Christ and Lord. And this will be a sign for you:
you will find an infant wrapped in swaddling clothes

and lying in a manger." And suddenly there was a multitude of
the heavenly host with the angel, praising God and saying:
"Glory to God in the highest and on earth peace to those on
whom his favor rests."

One of the great blessings of Immaculate Conception Church is the stunning stained-glass windows. Have you ever noticed a very curious thing about stained-glass? There are always two sides of a stained-glass window: a side where the light is, and the other side where it's dark. Obviously, those who enjoy stained-glass the most are those who are on the dark side of the windows. For instance, when it's dark outside, and we sit inside a beautiful church with all the lights on inside, there is more light on our side of the windows and less light on the outside. So, who can see the windows in all their brilliant colors? All those people outside, who are still looking for a parking space because they arrived late for Mass. Again, what would happen if we turned off all the lights in the church? Obviously, we would be sitting in the dark, and there would be more light from street lights outside than there is inside. As a result, we would be able to gaze upon the brilliant colors of the windows, while those outside would only see the dull gray and black panes of the windows. Curious, isn't it? If you ask me, that's the real beauty of stained-glass: It doesn't just have rich, vibrant saints and symbols for us to study and imitate; it also tells you who is in the dark and who is in the light. These brilliant stained-glass windows were specifically designed to help those who walk in the darkness, to give those in the dark much needed light and hope. The stained-glass windows are really created for those who walk in the dark.

The Scripture readings above speak about light and darkness, too, and you might say that these very Scripture passages function much like stained-glass because they, too, help those in the darkness, giving them light and hope. What do I mean? Isaiah prophesies in the first reading above, saying: "A people who walked in darkness have seen a great light; upon those who dwelt in a land of gloom a light has shone." So, if you asked Isaiah who's sitting in the dark, he'd say, "Everyone on earth is!" All humanity is sort of stumbling around in the dark, and that's why we are in dire need of a savior. Then, in the gospel an angel appears to shepherds at night, and St. Luke records what happened that original "o, dark thirty." Luke writes: "The angel of the Lord appeared to them and the glory of the Lord shone around them, and they were struck with great fear." Again, Luke points out that it is night, but he doesn't just mean it's physically night-time. He's also pointing to a spiritual darkness, too, which is why the shepherds were afraid. Do you ever become afraid in the dark? When Luke says the shepherds were afraid, he means they suffered from a spiritual darkness and were in need of a spiritual light to scatter their fear. The Scriptures above function kind of like the stunning stained-glass of Immaculate Conception Church, first of all proclaiming to the world that it is shrouded in darkness and fear, but second, and more important, assuring us we need not be afraid because the Light of the world is coming, the baby born in Bethlehem.

Now, let me ask you a very important question: Where is Jesus, the Light of the world, today? Obviously, Jesus is in the Church, in you and me, and in all Christians. After all, Jesus said to His disciples, "You are the light of the world. A city built on a hill cannot be hidden. Neither do people light a lamp and put it under a basket. Instead they put it on its stand, and it gives light to everyone in the house" (Matthew 5:14-15). So, clearly the Church is the light, and the rest of the world walks in darkness. A priest friend of mine said, "If you don't believe in original sin, just walk the streets of New York City." He works in the Bronx and sees the darkness caused by sin, where the Church tries to bring the light of Christ. Archbishop Fulton Sheen observed: "We are living at the end of Christendom, not at the end of Christianity, but at the end of Christendom." What he meant was that Christian ideas and ideals no longer guide and permeate our culture like they once did. Our world is plunging into a kind of spiritual night. So, Christians are in the light, and everyone else is in the dark. Right?

Not so fast. Sometimes, we Christians, and even we professional Christians — deacons, priests and bishops — prefer the darkness to the light of Christ. With our sins and our stupidity, our stumbles and our scandals, we grope around in the dark. Like a church building that is darkened when the lights are turned off, sometimes the light shines brighter outside than it does inside the Church. I believe one reason people love Pope Francis so much is because he's kind of like a stained-glass window for us as a Church, telling us that sometimes we Catholics are the ones sitting in the dark and overcome by our fears. That's why he's hired PR firms like McKinsey & Company, and international auditing agencies like Ernst and Young, to shine light on the darkness of Vatican finances, bringing transparency. He's exposing to the light of day any corruption hidden in the hierarchy and/or veiled behind false piety. He's calling all Christians to love the poor with a passion not seen since another Francis walked the roads of Rome, and fell in love with Lady Poverty. You see, the effect that Pope Francis is having on the Church is exactly how stained-glass works: It's not just pretty painted glass; it's a terrifying reminder of who's sitting in the darkness and who walks in the light.

I have an annoying little habit when I greet someone in Spanish. I always say, "Buenas noches." Now, that does not mean "good nachos!" It means, "Good night." I say that even when I meet someone in the middle of the day. Most Hispanics smile when I say that and think, "Oh, poor Fr. John, still learning Spanish. He hasn't learned how to say 'Good morning' yet." But I explain to them that I mean those words spiritually, that is, in comparison to Jesus the light, everything else — even the blazing sun at noonday — is like darkness. That's how bright the light of Christ is. When the book of Revelation describes heaven, it says, "They will not need the light of a lamp or the light of the sun, for the Lord God will give them light" (Revelations 22:5). That light is Jesus. In heaven, Jesus' light is so brilliant and blinding that it would even make the light of our sun look like darkness. Those two little words, "Buenas noches," are like a little stained-glass window reminding us that only Jesus is the light, and everything else, even the sun itself, is darkness compared to Him.

Each year as we celebrate Christmas, we remember that Jesus is the Light of the world. Now, that's the easy and enjoyable part of the Christmas story. The hard and humbling part is figuring out, as His light shines upon us, who might be sitting in the light and who is still stumbling in the dark.

SIRACH'S COMPASS

Navigating through the complexity of life

•••

Sirach 15:15-20

If you choose you can keep the commandments,

they will save you; if you trust in God, you too shall live;

he has set before you fire and water to whichever

you choose, stretch forth your hand.

Before man are life and death, good and evil,

whichever he chooses shall be given him.

Immense is the wisdom of the Lord;

he is mighty in power, and all-seeing.

The eyes of God are on those who fear him;

he understands man's every deed.

No one does he command to act unjustly,

to none does he give license to sin.

My high school composition teacher taught me the most important rule of writing. He called it the "KISS rule" which is an acronym for "keep it simple, stupid." The simpler, the sharper, the more concisely you can make your point, the more effective you'll be as a writer or a speaker. Many people who have to give a presentation worry about the wrong thing. They fretfully ask: "What am I going to say?" But it's quite easy to ramble on; it's much harder to be short and sweet. Mark Twain humorously quipped, "I didn't have time to write you a short letter, so I wrote a long one instead." Shakespeare said succinctly, "Brevity is the soul of wit" (*Hamlet*, II, 2). You can say more with less. Here's the catch: Being simple is hard; it's easier to be rootless and rambling, long and laborious. Heard any homilies like that? Heck, I've not only heard them, I've delivered them! How do you think I feel?

In the Scripture above, Sirach applies the KISS rule to the moral life, how to make good choices. Simplicity doesn't just help you write better, it helps you live better. Listen to the simple wisdom of Sirach. He writes: "God has set before you fire and water, to whichever you choose, stretch forth your hand." Even a child could catch Sirach's wisdom: Your hand should reach for water rather than fire. Then Sirach gets even more simple and straightforward, saying, "Before man are life and death, good and evil, whichever he chooses shall be given him." Sirach could not have made matters more plain: Morality is simple. Your hand should reach for water rather than fire; learn to choose life rather than death, good over evil. Keep it simple, stupid.

But as Mark Twain paradoxically pointed out, "simple" rarely means "easy." It's harder to write a short and sweet letter but much easier to write a longer and rambling one. In the same way, keeping moral choices simple and straightforward is extremely hard — life is usually far more complex. How often have politicians vigorously defended traditional marriage between one man and one woman? But when one of their own children declares he or she is gay, they change their political opinion. It's not so black and white. How simple it is to protest abortion, until you are the young woman facing an unplanned pregnancy. There's a fierce rivalry between Northside Grizzlies and Southside Rebels. What happens when a Rebel girl falls in love with a Grizzly boy? Suddenly, north and south are not polar opposites. Circumstances shouln't alter our morals but they can certainly make us more empathetic and challenge us.

So, what should we do? Throw out the KISS rule? Ignore Sirach's age-old wisdom? Capitulate to our culture that claims, "That may be true for you, but it's not true for me!" or those who say, "Don't impose your morality on me!" No, we can't cave in to our culture. Instead, I suggest we read Sirach not as a take-it-or-leave-it ultimatum, not with the mindset that everything is black and white, not so much as a commandment, but more like a compass that helps us find true north — Jesus. In other words, in navigating the moral life, Sirach gives us a compass that keeps us always oriented toward Jesus. I don't know about you, but I've taken plenty of detours in life and driven foolishly fast down dead-end roads, veering off the "straight and narrow." It's hard to be right, but so easy to be wrong. Aristotle, the ancient Greek philosopher, wisely said: "It is possible to fail in many ways, while to succeed is possible only in one way (for which reason also one is easy and the other difficult — to miss the mark easy, to hit it difficult). ... For men are good in but one way, but bad in many" (*Nicomachean Ethics*, II, 6). If you keep Sirach's compass handy, however, you won't get permanently lost no matter how lonely or abandoned you feel, no matter how many times or how tragically you've failed. Sirach's compass orients you back toward Christ.

By the way, you never need a compass more than when you're driving around Fort Smith, Ark.. As I drive around town, I can never tell which way is north and south, which way is east or west! I often get lost going to my parishioners' homes for supper, and have ended up at their neighbor's homes by mistake. (They are very nice people, by the way.) Growing up, I was always taught the Arkansas River flows east and west, but in Fort Smith, it runs north and south! Do you know what I use as my compass to find my bearings in Fort Smith? It's the church building itself. Before Vatican II, almost all churches were built on an east-west axis line. Do you know why? Because priests were required to say Mass "ad orientem," or "toward the east," toward the rising sun, which is how Jesus is described in the Bible. That's why our steeple is so tall. It's not because we're competing with the Baptists or Presbyterians or Methodists, but because we want people to use the church — not just the building but the whole universal Church — as their spiritual and moral compass, guiding them when they become lost. Whether I get lost in Fort Smith, or begin to wander in the moral desert of sin, I take out my compass, the Church — the "upgraded version" of Sirach's compass for today — and I can locate Jesus again and start inching my way back to Him.

So, was this homily long and rambling or short and sweet? Don't worry, I know the answer. Life is like that too: not short and sweet, not black and white, but gray and messy, complicated and confusing. When, sooner or later, you get lost on the journey of life, what you'll really need is a good compass.

THE REST OF THE STORY
Immersing ourselves into the lives of others and of God

• • •

EXODUS 34:4B-6, 8-9

Early in the morning Moses went up Mount Sinai
as the Lord had commanded him, taking along the
two stone tablets.
Having come down in a cloud, the Lord stood with Moses
there and proclaimed his name, "Lord."
Thus the Lord passed before him and cried out,
"The Lord, the Lord, a merciful and gracious God,
slow to anger and rich in kindness and fidelity."
Moses at once bowed down to the ground in worship.
Then he said, "If I find favor with you, O Lord,
do come along in our company.

2 CORINTHIANS 13:11-13

Brothers and sisters, rejoice.
Mend your ways, encourage one another,
agree with one another, live in peace,
and the God of love and peace will be with you.
Greet one another with a holy kiss.

All the holy ones greet you.

The grace of the Lord Jesus Christ.

JOHN 3:16-18

God so loved the world that he gave his only Son,

so that everyone who believes in him might not perish

but might have eternal life. For God did not send his Son

into the world to condemn the world, but that the world

might be saved through him.

Whoever believes in him will not be condemned.

Recently, I was talking to a psychologist friend of mine who works with priests in treatment. He shared with me the four most wonderful words you can ever say to someone: "Tell me your story." Has anyone ever said that to you? How refreshing to have someone to listen with sincere interest and compassion to our story. He always begins his initial counseling session that way, and he's amazed how eagerly and enthusiastically priests will share their life story with him. You see, most of the time we priests are on the other side of the counseling couch, giving our undivided attention to you. Rarely do we have such luxurious attention lavished on us, and so we really eat it up! But something more happens when we recount our life story than simply a personal history lesson. Sharing one's life story brings healing and wholeness, and even more, a sense of closeness and communion with the person who listens to our story. I am convinced that some of the world's deepest wounds fester because no one listens to another person's story.

Someone who cleverly capitalized on these four magic words was Jerry Jones. One of our parishioners attended a Dallas Cowboys football game in the new Cowboys Stadium, sometimes called "the Cowboy Cathedral" or the "Death Star" because the Cowboys' symbol is a star. This parishioner had the chance to meet Jerry Jones, the owner of the

Cowboys, and he described that rare and riveting encounter. Jones came up to him and sort of leaned back, sizing him up from top to bottom, and asked, "So, what's your story?" My friend was so moved by those wonderful words that he threw his arms around Jerry Jones' neck, and said emotionally, "I love you, man!" Then, he composed himself and stuttered something about loving the Cowboys. It was just those four simple words, "Tell me your story," that elicited such an effusive response. It didn't hurt that it was Jerry Jones who asked, of course.

The annual celebration of the feast of the Most Holy Trinity invites us to ponder the great mystery of our God who is Father, Son and Holy Spirit. But instead of explaining any one of today's readings, I want to say something about all three readings, and really why we have three readings every Sunday. The early Church Fathers, especially Gregory Nazianzen, saw the whole history of salvation — from creation to Christ's return — divided up into three great epochs or periods, each period highlighting the work of One of the Persons of the Trinity. So, the Old Testament speaks of the work of God the Father. The four gospels of Matthew, Mark, Luke and John are obviously about Jesus, the Son. And the rest of the New Testament — from Acts of the Apostles to the last book, Revelation — chronicle the work of the Spirit in the Church. In other words, the entire Bible is the life story of the three Persons of the Holy Trinity written large across the curtain of the cosmos. This is the reason at every Sunday Mass, we have three readings: one from the Old Testament, one from the New Testament and one from the Gospels. In those three readings, we hear about the involvement of the Father, and of the Son and of the Spirit in these periods of history corresponding to these three parts of the Bible. You see, when we read the Bible at Mass, and listen with undivided attention, it's as if we're saying to God, "Tell me your story!" And He does; God deeply desires to share His story with us, who He is and how much He loves us.

The reading of Scripture is not some stale history lesson about dead people and buried cities. When God shares His story with us, we are drawn into that story and become part of it. We enjoy a closeness and communion with God, analogous to that closeness between a counselor and client, but only in this case, the healing and wholeness are received by the listener, you and me. Like my friend meeting Jerry Jones and wanting to throw his arms around the storyteller and say, "I love you, man!" so too, the Mass moves from the ambo to the altar, from the Holy Bible to Holy Communion. Storytelling leads directly and deliberately to closeness and communion. Radio news commentator Paul Harvey always ended his news reports with the words, "And that, is the rest of the story." Well, when we listen to Scripture, the story of the Trinity, we are caught up into that terrific, timeless tale, we commune with God, and we become "the rest of God's story." All that transpires when someone says those four simple words: "Tell me your story."

I get very excited about a ministry at our church called "refugee resettlement." The United States Conferences of Bishops, together with the United Nations and the U.S. State Department, collaborated to develop a program in which a parish could help resettle a refugee family in the United States. When the bishop asked if any pastor would be interested, I enthusiastically answered, "Sure, we'll do it! There's nothing going on around here!" Our first family was from Iraq: a mom and dad, and a 4-year-old daughter. Why are we doing this? Well, because of what Emma Lazarus wrote at the base of the Statue of Liberty, proudly proclaiming what we Americans do best. You know the words, "Give me your tired, your poor, your huddled masses yearning to be free; the wretched refuse of your teeming shore. Send these, the tempest-tossed to me, I lift my lamp beside the golden door." There's another reason we do this, which is an even more important reason. That is because that Iraqi family also had a story to tell, and I wanted to hear that story and share it. You see, when we say to another person, "Tell me your story," we bring about healing and wholeness, communion and close-ness, and we begin to heal those wounds that fester in the very heart of humanity.

The four most wonderful words in the world are "Tell me your story." Every Sunday, the Scriptures tell us God's story, transforming us in the exchange. This coming week, say those magic words to someone else, and become part of their story. Let me warn you: These words have a peculiar power. After you utter them, don't be surprised if that person suddenly throws their arms around you and sobs, "I love you, man!"

TWENTY MINUTES OF HELL

Moderating our expectations in doing God's will

•••

MATTHEW 2:13-15, 19-23

When the magi had departed, behold,

the angel of the Lord appeared to Joseph in a dream and said,

"Rise, take the child and his mother, flee to Egypt, and stay

there until I tell you.

Herod is going to search for the child to destroy him."

Joseph rose and took the child and his mother by night

and departed for Egypt.

He stayed there until the death of Herod, that what the Lord had

said through the prophet might be fulfilled,

Out of Egypt I called my son.

When Herod had died, behold,

the angel of the Lord appeared in a dream

to Joseph in Egypt and said,

"Rise, take the child and his mother and go to the land of Israel,

for those who sought the child's life are dead."

He rose, took the child and his mother,

and went to the land of Israel.

But when he heard that Archelaus was ruling over Judea

> in place of his father Herod,
>
> he was afraid to go back there.
>
> And because he had been warned in a dream,
>
> he departed for the region of Galilee.
>
> He went and dwelt in a town called Nazareth,
>
> so that what had been spoken
>
> through the prophets might be fulfilled,
>
> He shall be called a Nazorean."

I want to tell you a secret. The secret is how to tell a really good movie from a movie that stinks. You don't have to read the movie reviews in the newspaper or listen to them online; forget all that. This may surprise you, but whether a movie is good or not has very little to do with the movie itself. Rather, it has everything to do with us, with our expectations of how good or bad we think the movie will be. Whenever I walk into a movie that's really hyped-up, presented as "the blockbuster hit of the year" (which they all are), what invariably happens? I am disappointed; it's a let down. No matter how good the acting or the plot or the special effects, my sky-high expectations have doomed the movie to failure before I gulp my second handful of popcorn. On the other hand, when I've walked into a movie with little hope of enjoying it, usually because a priest friend dragged me to it, I've always been surprised and ended up enjoying it. Has this ever happened to you? So often, our unduly high expectations cloud our appreciation of enjoying a movie.

I'll never forget one of the first comments that Mike Anderson made when he was hired as the head basketball coach of the Arkansas Razorbacks. Being a Nolen Richardson protégé, Anderson inherited very high expectations from fans, which he tried to bring down to earth. He said, "I know Razorback fans are hoping for that famous 40 minutes of hell. Well, this first year, it will be more like 20 minutes of hell, and 20 minutes of I don't know what the hell we're doing!" The

Razorbacks have gotten better and better each year, but that first year Anderson had to lower people's expectations. Great expectations don't always lead to great results.

In the gospel above, we see someone else who understood the perils of high expectations, St. Joseph. Every time Joseph shows up in the Scriptures, an angel of God appears and tells him to do something completely unexpected. Joseph, like any newly married man, had great hopes and dreams for his budding family, but they were all dashed. First, an angel tells Joseph not to worry about taking Mary as his wife, even though she was pregnant with a baby that was not his. Can you imagine the anguish Joseph must have felt? But Joseph obeys. Then, an angel tells Joseph to take the baby and his wife and move to Egypt, where Joseph knew no one and had no means to provide for his family. Again, Joseph complies with silent assent. Finally, an angel directs Joseph to return to Israel just as the Holy Family was adjusting to life in a foreign country. Again and again, Joseph is directed to something entirely unexpected, and quite often humiliating and even dangerous. Does Joseph complain? Does he shake a defiant fist at heaven and yell, "This isn't what I signed up for!" That's what you and I would do, but not Joseph. You could say Joseph was experiencing "40 minutes of hell" all right, not because he was dishing it out, but because he was humbly taking it. How many married couples do you hear say, "If I'd known then what I know now, I never would have gotten married"? Not St. Joseph. Joseph understood that sometimes you have to forego your own "great expectations" and humbly accept God's plans and promises.

I don't want you to misunderstand my message. It's not that our hopes and dreams are so great, and that God's plans for us are puny and we just have to settle for less, be content with the mediocre. It's actually the other way around: not that we think too big, but that our expectations are too small. In his celebrated essay *The Weight of Glory*, C.S. Lewis helps us see the difference between God's expectations and our own. Lewis writes: "We are half-hearted creatures, fooling around with drink and sex and ambition when infinite joy is offered us, [we are] like an ignorant child who wants to go on making mud pies in a slum because he cannot imagine what is meant by the offer of a holiday at the sea. We are too easily pleased." In other words, we want too little, not too much. God's hopes and dreams for us are so great we can hardly imagine them; instead, we settle for our mud pies in the slum.

What are your expectations? Do you have high hopes, big plans, ambitious dreams? Do you hope to cure cancer someday? Wonderful. Do you want to set a new world record in snowboarding? Great. Do you dream of being the richest man or woman in the world? Go for it! Maybe some of you are setting your sights on something a little less glamorous: You just want your kids to avoid drugs, you'd like to avoid a divorce, you'd like to have a stable job, you'd like your parents not to get cancer, maybe you just want to graduate from sixth grade! These are all good and reasonable expectations for our lives.

Whatever your expectations, however, always remember two things. First, don't assume that what you want is what God wants. Joseph found out the difference between the two the hard way, but he humbly accepted it. Isaiah the prophet reminds us: "My ways are as high above your ways as the sky is above the earth" (Isaiah 55:9). I love that old saying, "If you want to make God laugh, just tell him your plans." It's not because God delights in our downfall. No, exactly the opposite is true: He wants to give us far more than we can imagine. That's the second thing: God always wants to give you more than what you hoped for, not less. St. John of the Cross, the Carmelite mystic who gave up everything worldly to follow God, summed up his teaching in three Spanish words, "Nada, nada, nada." Do you know what that means? It means: "Nothing, nothing, nothing." Wow, what a depressing life; that sounds really boring and morbid, right? Wrong! Through prayer and patience and perseverance, John learned what Joseph knew: It's only by forfeiting everything this world has to offer — really, our unrealistic expectations of this world — that you can grab hold of everything God wants to offer you. John didn't really want "nada," he wanted everything.

Next time you want to invite me to go see a movie with you, here's what you do: Tell me the movie stinks, it's the worst movie ever, they should pay us to go see it. I'll be happy to drive. It is often wise to reign in our expectations about life in general, too. Because sometimes, life is 20 minutes of hell, and sometimes it's just 20 minutes of "I don't know what the hell we're doing!"

WHO MOVED MY CHEESE?

Embracing the change necessary for growth

•••

JOHN 6:41-51

The Jews murmured about Jesus because he said,

"I am the bread that came down from heaven," and they said,

"Is this not Jesus, the son of Joseph?

Do we not know his father and mother?

Then how can he say, 'I have come down from heaven?'"

Jesus answered and said to them,

"Stop murmuring among yourselves.

No one can come to me unless the Father who sent

me draw him, and I will raise him on the last day.

It is written in the prophets:

They shall all be taught by God. Everyone who listens to my

Father and learns from him comes to me.

Not that anyone has seen the Father except the one who

is from God; he has seen the Father.

Amen, amen, I say to you, whoever believes has eternal life.

I am the bread of life.

Your ancestors ate the manna in the desert, but they died;

this is the bread that comes down from heaven

so that one may eat it and not die.

I am the living bread that came down from heaven;

whoever eats this bread will live forever;

and the bread that I will give

is my flesh for the life of the world."

The best little book I've ever read on dealing with change is called *Who Moved My Cheese?* by Spencer Johnson. Change is hard. We get used to our routine and expect life to unfold neatly according to our schedule. It often doesn't, does it? It's painful to adapt to change. I'm the world's worst at changing. A few years ago, I was debating my brother about reading old books versus embracing new technology. I said, "Look, basically Plato and Aristotle said it all, and we're just rehashing what they said." Well, my brother remarked, "John, you just like things that are old fashioned." I replied, "No, Paul, I like things that are eternal." When you don't want something to change, just call it "eternal."

Who Moved My Cheese? is for stick-in-the-mud people like me who don't like to change. It's about four characters living in a maze looking for cheese, which they love. Two of them are mice named Sniff and Scurry, and two are little people the size of mice named Hem and Haw. One day the cheese they had all been enjoying is all gone and they have to deal with the reality of no cheese. The two mice, Sniff and Scurry, quickly adapt to the change and hurry off into the maze to find new cheese. Hem and Haw, as their names suggest, just sit there and complain about their cheeseless situation. The rest of the story is about how Haw learns to deal with change. First, he learns to face his fears. He asks himself, "What would you do if you weren't afraid?" A powerful question. Second, he learns to laugh at his stubbornness and shortsightedness. And third, he finally enjoys the adventure of searching for new cheese. Poor, Hem, on the other hand, is left still sitting and sulking back in Cheeseless Station C, like me reading old books and dreaming about old cheese. You have to change to find the new cheese.

In the gospel above, Jesus invites the Jews to adapt to change in their faith. He doesn't talk about losing old cheese and finding new cheese; instead, He explains the difference between old manna and the New Manna, namely, Himself. Our Lord explains, "Your ancestors ate the manna in the desert, but they died; this is the bread that comes down from heaven so that one may eat it and not die." Then comes the clincher: Jesus says, "I am the bread that comes down from heaven." How did the Jews react? Just like the four characters in the book about cheese. The holy women and apostles were like Sniff and Scurry quickly adapting and chasing the New Manna. Nicodemus the Pharisee and Joseph of Arimethea were like Haw, slowly but surely seeing the need to change and chase the new cheese, Jesus. Most of the Sanhedrin, however, were like Hem: old fuddy duddies like me, hemmed in by their old traditions and stubbornly sticking to their old manna. You have to change if you want to find the new cheese.

A while back, I gave the invocation at the Arkansas Association of Counties, with Governor Mike Beebe present. I took a chance and started with a joke about the governor. I said, "Several months ago Governor Beebe was scheduled to speak at a city in another state. He drove around the unfamiliar downtown desperately looking for a parking space, because he was already late, but didn't find one. The governor looked up to heaven and said this sincere prayer. "Dear Lord, have pity on me. If you help me find a parking place, I promise I'll never miss another Sunday service, and I won't touch another drop of alcohol ever again." All of a sudden, miraculously, a parking space opened up right before the governor's eyes. He quickly looked up to heaven again and said, "Never mind, Lord, I found one myself." Fortunately, the governor was laughing like everyone else. As he came up to deliver his address, he looked over at me and winked. I didn't have the heart to tell him that I didn't vote for him in the last election. That was the first time I saw Governor Beebe in person, and I liked him. I could tell he would be a lot like Haw: He could laugh at himself; he didn't take himself too seriously. Maybe that's why he's been a good governor to lead our state through so much economic turmoil and change. If you want to find the new cheese, you have to change.

My friends, I hate to tell you this, but change happens. What's worse, you are powerless to prevent it. However, how we react to that change is within our power: We can Hem and Haw about the change or we can Sniff and Scurry and rise to the new challenges. Some struggle against the changes in technology — iPhone, iPads, Nooks and Kindles — and believe that all modern technology is the work of the devil. Others embrace the change. Recently, Pope Benedict sent his first papal tweet. Sometimes the changes come more personally and permanently: the death of a loved one, a broken marriage, a ruptured relationship, a serious illness like cancer, the loss of a job, starting a new school. The pain can be so piercing it paralyzes you. It's still change, and our options are still the same. Anyone who lived through the Second Vatican Council in the 1960s and 1970s will tell you it felt like the whole Church changed overnight. It did change a lot, but not in what was essential, not in what was eternal. Like Jesus teaching the Jews to let go of the old manna and taste the new, so the pope and the bishops invited Catholics to let go of the old Mass and accept the new. I'm sure it will change again.

I don't know why change happens, especially the really hard kind. I don't know why God "moves our cheese" just as we're settling down to enjoy it. The best reaction to change is prayer, and the best prayer to face change with was written by American theologian Reinhold Nieburhr. It goes: "God, grant me the serenity to accept the things I cannot change, the courage to change the things I can; and the wisdom to know the difference." Most people don't know, however, the prayer continues, and the second part is even better: "Living one day at a time;

enjoying one moment at a time; accepting hardships as the pathway to peace, take, as He (meaning Jesus) did, this sinful world as it is, not as I would have it; trusting that He will make all things right if I surrender to His will; that I may be reasonably happy in this life and supremely happy with Him forever in the next. Amen."

By the way, last month, my brother gave me one of those fancy new tablets for my birthday. I'm proud to say, I've almost got it unwrapped.

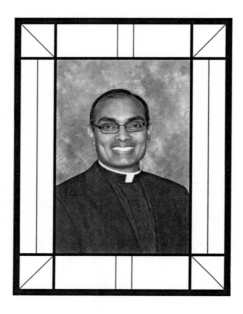

Rev. John K. Antony, born in New Delhi, India, emigrated to the United States when he was 7 years old and grew up in Little Rock, Ark. In 1991, he graduated magna cum laude from the University of Dallas, was ordained a Catholic priest in Arkansas in 1996, and later completed a licentiate degree in Canon Law. He currently serves as pastor of Immaculate Conception Church in Fort Smith, Ark., as well as a judge on the Court of Second Instance for marriage annulment cases. He has also served as the Diocesan Director of Vocations for four years. Rev. Antony has received popular acclaim for his ability to communicate the sometimes complex truths of Christianity in a way that is both human and humorous. This is his first book.

CPSIA information can be obtained at www.ICGtesting.com
Printed in the USA
BVOW05*1808101114

374462BV00002B/6/P